THE CONFESSIONS OF
PSYCHOPATHS

THE CONFESSIONS OF
PSYCHOPATHS
THEIR EVIL CRIMES TOLD
IN THEIR OWN WORDS

AL CIMINO

Al Cimino is a journalist and author who specialises in the genres of true crime and military history. His most recent titles include *War in the Pacific, Nazi Sex Spies, Women who Kill: A Chilling Casebook of True-Life Murders, The Story of the SS: Hitler's Infamous Legions of Death* and *21st-Century Psychos: The Most Horrifying Killers of the Modern Era*. He lives in London in the UK.

This edition published in 2025 by Arcturus Publishing Limited
26/27 Bickels Yard, 151–153 Bermondsey Street,
London SE1 3HA

AD011902UK
Supplier 40, Date 0825, PI 00011643

Printed in the UK

Authorised Representative:
Easy Access System Europe - Mustamäe tee 50, 10621 Tallinn, Estonia
gpsr.requests@easproject.com

Contents

A Warning

Normally, when I write books about psychopaths and serial killers, I include as much material as I can about their victims. They, after all, are the important ones, not the deranged scumbags who robbed them of their – often innocent, young – lives. That is not possible here as the killer usually did not know the victim. Nor did they want to, in most cases only learning their name later in the media. Otherwise, as they say, it would make the murder 'too personal'. So, as we have here only the serial killers' words, there is nothing much to be said about the victims, nothing to hide behind.

And the words are grisly in the extreme. This is not a book for the faint-hearted. These killers seem to relish the gruesome details of the vile things they have done, even when trying to excuse themselves. With what is reported here, we are effectively seeing the most hideous crimes through the killers' own eyes.

A second warning. There is a great deal of explicit sex in this book. Sex is, after all, the principal motivation for the psychopathic killer. And it is not cosy, warm, tender, loving sex. It is sex of the most brutal, disgusting and gut-wrenching kind.

I could not spare the details. That would somehow prettify the abominable acts of perpetrators, making them more acceptable. It is said that God hates the sin and loves the sinner. That's his or her prerogative, but it is hard for reasonable human beings to be so forgiving. Nevertheless, if we are going to hear the words of these killers, they are not going to smarten them up for us or take the edge off. They are not going to pull a punch, as it were. By their very nature, these killers are brutal and offensive. It should be remembered that even the hardened detectives who interrogate these fiends often seek counselling.

Given that we are about to sink into the deepest, darkest pits of depravity, it is perhaps unnecessary to mention that some of the characters in this book have the attitudes and language of their times. They do not reflect those of the author.

That said, *bon voyage* on the journey of the damned.

Introduction

The confessions in this book come from many different sources. Some are the admissions made to the police when the killer was finally caught. There is testimony given by the killer in court. Killers talk to journalists and authors. Some write their own memoir. Others own up to their monstrous crimes in correspondence.

These confessions should not be taken at face value. Some killers try to find some specious justification for their actions. 'God made me do it.' 'I was possessed by an evil spirit.' 'It was not my fault.' Or maybe the excuse was that they were gripped by an irresistible urge and could not resist it.

Of course, this may just be self-serving. The killer may be trying to find mitigation to avoid the death penalty. Or they may be trying to convince the authorities that they are insane and end up in a relatively cosy mental hospital rather than a dank and draughty penitentiary. That way, there is some slim chance that, after a handful of years, the doctors may claim they are cured and set them free. Or they may really be nuts. It is hard to believe that the people that do the diabolical things described in this book are truly sane. Remember that sanity in this context has a legal rather than a medical definition – did the perpetrator know right from wrong? Can they be held responsible for their actions? In the cases here, it has been adjudged that they were sane within the meaning of the law.

Even the vilest fiend sometimes worries about what family and friends – and other human beings – think. Even in jail they are surrounded by other people. They depend on the good offices of the prison staff. There is also what other prisoners think of you to consider. After all, you are probably going to be around them for the rest of your life.

While telling all to a police interrogator, you have to consider the impression you are making on them, even if you are playing the devil incarnate. Don't forget, they are going to give testimony about you in court. Your life is in their hands to some extent. Like it or not, you are going to have to consider what impact your words are going to have on the judge and jury. Even the most egotistical of us are conscious in some small way of the opinions of others and a courtroom is a place where people are judged. You can't just walk out if people don't like what you are saying.

The same applies if you are giving your confession to a journalist or a writer. They are going to give their testimony in the court of public opinion. If you didn't care, why would you speak to them? And in memoirs or letters, you are in some way trying to influence the thoughts and feelings of the reader. Again, why bother if it didn't matter to you what they thought of you? We are social beings and we can't help being influenced by others and seeking to influence them.

Some killers are bewildered by what they have done and why they have done it, and want to get it off their chest. They want to work through it by spelling it out to a sympathetic listener. It could be considered a kind of informal therapy.

Then, there are those who relish the retelling and get a kick from reliving the moment. They spend their time in prison savouring every detail of their atrocious actions. Killing gave them such a kick that they want to go over and over it in their mind as if it were their life's work, the one thing that gave meaning to their existence on this planet. Born without a talent, they weren't going to be a great actor, artist, writer or pop star. Nor did a career in politics or the media beckon.

Being a serial killer has made them infamous and they revel in it. Before they started killing, they were an anonymous nobody. Then their crimes got them into the newspapers. At first, the murders were reported one by one. Then came the revelation that a serial killer was on the prowl.

The general public were alarmed. They follow every twist and turn of the investigation. Then, you begin to inhabit their nightmares. Hundreds of detectives are called in to hunt you down. For a while, you are clever enough to outwit them. Though you have to keep it to yourself, for once you are aglow with self-esteem.

Then, you are caught. But you are still the star of the show. The police want to interview you at length. They want to know every detail. They may even take you out around the various crime scenes where press photographers and TV cameramen will catch a glimpse of you. And there are lawyers to brief. As you are their client, they are obliged to take an interest in you, even if they are only the public defender. Another boost for your ego.

At the trial, you are the main attraction. Everything that goes on involves you or is about you. When the jury goes out to deliberate, there is only one thing on their minds. Even after sentencing when you are banged up, psychologists and detectives from the FBI's Behavioral Science Unit – later the Behavioral Analysis Unit – want to study you.

People will want to write books, like this one, about you. And there's even a chance that you might become a TV star. There is an endless appetite for documentaries about serial killers on various streaming platforms. After all, let's face it, once you are seen to be a serial killer, no other career path is going to be open to you. There may be another brief burst of publicity if you kill someone – or are killed by someone – in jail. But killing and being a serial killer is what defines you. That's it.

On the other hand, there are those who simply do not give a damn – those who simply hate the world and everyone in it, including themselves, and would go on and on killing if they could. They make a chilling existential statement that challenges everything we hold dear. They possess the grim fascination of a Hitler who, eight decades after his death, is still the subject of numerous books, films and documentaries because no one can figure him out. How could anyone have done what he did? So, why do they bother to make a confession? It is not an attempt to explain themselves. Rather it is a spit in the face of the public.

But we must not consider these psychopaths as media stars, even though they often think that of themselves. They are disgusting human beings who do the most detestable things – as you are about to discover. (I'm running out of disagreeable adjectives.) Indeed, as you read their own words, you may wonder whether they are human beings at all. It is not my place to give you any guidance here. You decide.

CHAPTER ONE

Ted Bundy

Ted Bundy was a serial killer who confessed to the murders of 30 young women, largely students, often raping his victims and continuing to perform sex acts on their bodies after they were dead. He began his homicidal career in Washington state, moving on to Colorado, then Utah where he was jailed for aggravated kidnapping and attempted criminal assault. He was then sent back to face murder charges in Colorado, where he achieved notoriety by escaping twice. Heading for Florida, he continued his rampage. Convicted of three murders and a series of other offences, he died in the electric chair in Florida State Prison in 1989.

Although he denied everything up until very nearly the end, he left an extraordinary insight into the thought processes of a psychopath in interviews he gave to journalists, shrinks and the police, outbursts in courtrooms where he defended himself and things he said to his long-time girlfriend, Liz Kendall, and intended victims who eluded him.

Oftentimes, without admitting guilt, he would talk about himself in the third person, speculating on what an individual like him would have done in the given circumstances and, seeking to excuse himself, he blamed pornography.

Bundy said he began casually reading soft-core pornography when he was 12 or 13 years old. He and his friends found pornographic books in the garbage cans in his neighbourhood. 'From time to time, we would come across pornographic books of a harder nature... a more graphic, explicit nature than we would encounter at the local grocery store,' he told psychologist, James Dobson.

'The most damaging kinds of pornography,' he said, 'are those that involve violence and sexual violence. Because the wedding of those two forces, as I know only too well, brings out the hatred that is just too terrible to describe.'

A late starter at dating, Bundy insisted, 'He has no hatred for women… [but] he got sucked into the more sinister doctrines that are implicit in pornography – the use, the abuse, the possession of women as objects.'

Worse.

'A certain percentage of it is devoted toward literature that explores situations where a man, in the context of a sexual encounter, in one way or another engages in some sort of violence toward a woman, or the victim. Your girlfriend, your wife, a stranger, children – whatever – a whole host of victims is found in this kind of literature.'

It was a one-way street.

'But slowly, throughout the years, reading pornography began to become a deadly habit… Like an addiction, you keep craving something that is harder, something which gives you a greater sense of excitement. Until you reach a point where the pornography only goes so far, you reach that jumping-off point where you begin to wonder if maybe actually doing it would give you that which is beyond just reading or looking at it.'

Peeping Tom

While a student at the University of Puget Sound in Washington state in 1967, the 20-year-old Bundy started seeing his dream co-ed, known by the pseudonym, Diane Edwards.

'The relationship I had with Diane had a lasting impact on me,' he said, later adding she was 'the only woman I ever really loved'. At the same time, he was progressing from pornography to voyeurism.

'He was walking down the street one evening and just totally by chance looked up into the window of a house and saw a woman un-dressing,' Bundy told journalist Stephen G. Michaud, again referring to himself in the third person. 'He peeped in windows and watched women undress or whatever could be seen during the evening. He approached it almost like a project, throwing himself into it, literally for years.'

Then he began interfering with women's cars, in the hope that they might turn to him for help. 'It's kind of a game, sort of like, "Let's see how far it goes."'

Drinking played its part.

'When this person drank a good deal, his inhibitions were significantly diminished. He would find that his urge to engage in voyeuristic behaviour, or trips to the bookstore, would become more prevalent, more urgent... On every occasion he engaged in such behaviour, he was intoxicated.'

Things were about to take a dangerous turn.

Crossing the boundary

'On one particular evening,' he said, 'when he had been drinking a great deal, he was passing a bar where he saw a woman leave and walk up a fairly dark side street. Something seemed to seize him... Without a great deal of thought, he searched around for some instrumentality to attack this woman with. He found a piece of two-by-four in a lot and proceeded to follow and track this girl for several blocks.

'The situation was novel because, while he may have toyed around with fantasies before and made several abortive attempts to act out a fantasy, it never before had reached the point where actually he was confronted with harming another individual.'

But Bundy was determined to go through with it.

'So, he'd gotten ahead of his quarry, this girl, and was lying in wait for her. But before she reached the point where he was concealed, she turned and went into her house.'

It was a watershed.

'On succeeding evenings, he began to scurry around that same neighbourhood, obsessed with the image he had seen. On one particular occasion, he saw a woman park her car and walk up to her door and fumble for her keys. He walked up behind her and struck her with a piece of wood he was carrying. She fell down and began screaming. He panicked and ran.'

The experience terrified him. He had not realized that he was capable of doing such a thing.

It was the first time he felt that he had been possessed by 'something awful and alien. There is just absolutely no way to describe first the brutal urge to do that kind of thing…'

For the moment, he was determined to restrain himself.

'He sat back and swore to himself that he wouldn't do something like that again, or even anything that would lead to it. He did everything he should have done. He didn't go out at night, and when he was drinking, he stayed around friends. For a period of months, the enormity of what he did stuck with him…

'But slowly, the pressures, tensions, dissatisfactions, which, in the very early stages, fuelled this thing, had an effect. Gradually, it would re-emerge. This individual would say, "Well, just one trip to the bookstore. Just once around the neighbourhood."'

Inappropriate behaviour

Within six months, he had fallen back into his old routine. By then, Bundy was having a relationship with Liz Kendall. Her daughter, Molly, recalled that he was babysitting her when she was seven and they were playing hide-and-seek. She found him hiding under a blue blanket and, when she pulled it away, got a shock.

'You're naked!' she screamed.

'I know,' he said, 'but that's because I can turn invisible, but my clothes can't, and I didn't want you to see me!'

The pair wrestled. Molly said that, at the time, she did not know what an erection was. There were other incidents of inappropriate behaviour – and violence. When they went rafting, Bundy pushed Liz overboard and made no attempt to help her as she struggled to get back on board.

And he was stealing. When Liz noticed that he had a new television, stereo and typewriter, she accused him of being a thief. He grabbed her by her arm.

'If you ever tell anyone about this,' he said, 'I'll break your fucking neck.'

Then, young women began going missing in the area and it was thought that Bundy was responsible. But just as he referred to himself in the third person, he was loath to identify his victims.

'Then, on another night, he saw a woman walking home,' he said. 'He followed her and looked in the window and watched her get ready for bed. He did this on several occasions, for this was a regular kind of thing. Eventually, he created a plan where he would attack her. Early one morning, he sneaked in through a door he knew would be open and entered the bedroom. Implementing a plan… he jumped on the woman's bed and attempted to restrain her. All he succeeded in doing was waking her up and causing her to panic and scream. He left very rapidly.

'Then, he was seized with the same kind of disgust and repulsion and fear and wonder at why he was allowing himself to attempt such extraordinary violence. But the significance of this particular occasion was that, while he stayed off the streets and vowed he'd never do it again, it took him only three months to get over it.'

Vicious attack

This incident was far more serious than Bundy made out. The victim is thought to have been 18-year-old Karen Sparks, a dancer and student at Washington University, who lived in a basement room of a big, old house on 8th Avenue in the campus district of Seattle. On the morning of 4 January 1974, her housemates found her unconscious, her face covered with blood. She had been beaten round the head with a metal bar wrenched from the bed frame. When they pulled back the covers, they found it had been forced into her vagina, causing terrible internal damage.

She survived after more than a week in a coma. The blow to the head left her permanently brain-damaged. The police believed that she had been attacked by a Peeping Tom, who had seen her undressing though a basement window.

'What happened,' Bundy went on, 'was that this entity inside him was not capable of being controlled any longer.'

He dismissed anger or hostility as a motive. There was something else at play.

'The fantasy is always more stimulating than the aftermath of the crime itself,' he said. 'He should have recognized that what really fascinated him was the hunt, the adventure of searching out his victims. And, to a degree, possessing them physically, as one would possess a potted plant, a painting or a Porsche. Owning, as it were, this individual.'

Basement bloodbath

Bundy's first acknowledged victim was 21-year-old psychology student, Lynda Ann Healy, who lived just a few blocks away on 12th Avenue. She too had a bedroom in the basement and was attacked just one month later.

'He had seen the house before,' said Bundy, 'and for one reason or another had been attracted to its occupants. Then one evening, just being in the mood so to speak, he checked out the house... found the front door was open.'

Bundy was not clear as to whether he was carrying a weapon.

'I really don't know. If he had struck the woman, she probably would have left a large amount of blood. If she was stabbed, there also would be blood.'

On the morning of 1 February, Lynda was reported missing. When homicide detectives pulled back the bedclothes, they found blood had soaked through to the mattress. In the closet, they found Lynda's nightdress and the clothes she had been wearing the previous evening were missing, but Bundy was not forthcoming about what had happened.

'In that situation, a person who was alert enough to be able to dress would not be afraid in terms of struggling or crying out,' he said. 'So, it was unlikely that any attempt was made to clothe the girl.'

But it was not clear that she was unconscious.

'Walking out under her own power at that hour of the morning would not necessarily be the soundest kind of approach.'

And the made bed?

'It was an attempt to cover up her disappearance.'

Would the girl be bound with rope or some kind of restraint?

'[That] would be the way it was done,' Bundy said. 'He would have gagged the person.'

He would then have driven her to 'some place that was quiet and private. His home or some secluded area. It would depend upon the condition of the girl... It would depend on a person's state of mind. How calm or excited he was.'

Bundy conceded that he would not have been calm.

'This was one of the first instances that he'd abducted a woman in this fashion. He was extremely nervous, almost frantic, and in a panic trying to attempt anything. There you are, what do you do with the situation? He'd probably put her in the back seat of his car and cover her with something.

'Let's say he decided to drive to a remote location that he just picked out. Once he arrived at this point where he didn't have a fear of alarming anyone with shouts or screams or whatever, [he'd] untie the woman... He would have the girl undress.'

Bundy then raped her, though he did not use the word. Instead, he felt 'that part of himself gratified'.

But that was not the end of it.

'A certain amount of the need of that malignant condition had been satisfied through the sexual release. That driving force would recede somewhat… He realized he couldn't let the girl go. And at that point he would kill her and leave the body where he had taken her.'

So, how did he feel after his first murder?

'A nominally normal individual, who has become somewhat subordinate to bizarre desires and abducts a woman and kills her, finds himself in a great deal of panic… The tension was focused primarily on the progress of the police investigation. If nothing of any significance was disclosed in the newspapers, that would be one way the tension was reduced.'

Forensic examination of Healy's room came up with nothing. The perpetrator had not left so much as a hair, or a drop of blood or semen.

'As far as remorse over the act, that would last for a period of time,' said Bundy. 'He would say, "Well, listen. You fucked up this time, but you're never gonna do it again." But this didn't last for very long – a matter of weeks… As time passes, the emphasis is on, "Don't get caught."'

Rash of deaths

Next, 19-year-old Donna Manson, a student at Evergreen State College near Olympia in Washington, 60 miles (96 km) from Seattle, went missing on the night of 12 March 1974. Bundy claimed that he burned Manson's skull in his girlfriend's fireplace 'down to the last ash' in 'a fit of… paranoia and cleanliness'.

Then, 18-year-old Susan Elaine Rancourt disappeared from Central Washington State College in Ellensburg, 110 miles (177 km) southeast of Seattle on 17 April.

Bundy then moved out of state. On 6 May, 22-year-old Roberta Kathleen Parks went missing from Oregon State University in Corvallis.

'It would be an attempt to commit a crime without it being linked to other crimes,' Bundy said.

In the early hours of 1 June, 22-year-old Brenda Ball disappeared hitchhiking home from the Flame Tavern in Burien near the airport in southern Seattle. Eighteen-year-old Georgann Hawkins, a student at the University of Washington, left a party on 11 June to walk home. She never arrived.

'Parks disappeared in May, and Ball disappeared on June 1st, which is just a little less than a month,' Bundy said. 'Georgann Hawkins disappeared on the night of June 11th, which is just a few days after the Ball disappearance. So, we can see by the short period of time that elapsed between the disappearance of Parks and the disappearance of Ball that there would not be a great deal of change in the state of mind of the individual.'

With Kathy Parks, Bundy said, 'Let's say she was having a snack in the cafeteria and [he] just sat down next to her and began talking, and representing himself to be a student there, and suggested that they go out somewhere to get a bite to eat or to get a drink.'

Bundy was noted for his charm and good looks.

'A jog down to a local tavern in Corvallis would probably be the farthest he would expect her to accept as a plausible kind of trip… So, once [he] had gained her confidence, then on the way to this tavern they were going to go to, he said that he'd just remembered that he had to pick up the finished copy of his thesis or something from the typist, and then drove out to a remote location.'

A gun would not be necessary.

'This guy pulls up in a cornfield somewhere… Recognizing the disadvantage of [her position], she would submit to whatever instructions he gave her… let's say he had a preference to watch the victims undress.'

There followed what Bundy called a 'sexual encounter'.

Murder mountain

The bodies of Lynda Healy, Susan Rancourt, Kathy Parks and Brenda Ball were found on Taylor Mountain, some 20 miles (32 km) to the east of Seattle. Bundy said he had dumped Donna Manson's remains there, too. He also 'speculated' that Kathy Parks had been alive when she was driven back to Seattle and raped twice on the way.

'Ordinarily [he] would not want to inflict any unnecessary violence or pain to the girl. So it wasn't necessary to render her unconscious. He would have had only to tie her up.'

The journey back to Seattle would take five hours. Would he rape her again before he killed her?

'Well, given the amount of time they would have had to have been together, it's likely.'

The murder occurred on Taylor Mountain, where her body was found.

Bundy took pride in the fact that his technique was improving when he picked up Brenda Ball.

'He picked her up hitchhiking and they got to talking and she had nothing to do. He would ask her if she wanted to go to a party at his place and take her home. At this point, he would exert an influence on her, which would be especially effective if she was under the influence of alcohol.'

When they got to his place, she would discover that there was no party.

'The initial sexual encounter would be more or less a voluntary one, but one which did not wholly gratify the full spectrum of desires that he had intended,' he said. 'And so, after the first sexual encounter, gradually his sexual desire builds back up and joins, as it were, these other, unfulfilled desires, this other need to totally possess her. After she'd passed out, he strangled her to death.'

This did not explain why, when her skull was found on Taylor Mountain, the right side showed that it had sustained a traumatic blunt-force injury.

Getting away with it

Ten days after he had killed Brenda Ball, Bundy abducted Georgann Hawkins. His MO was to feign injury and ask for assistance to carry books or a briefcase back to his car. Then, he hit her with a crowbar, put her in the car and handcuffed her. As they drove to a new killing site at Issaquah, a little closer to Seattle than Taylor Mountain, she regained consciousness at one point.

'At this point, she was quite lucid,' Bundy said. Shortly after, he knocked her unconscious again and strangled her.

On 14 July 1974, Bundy abducted two women – 23-year-old Janice Ott and 19-year-old Denise Naslund – in broad daylight from a crowded beach at Lake Sammamish State Park in Issaquah.

'There were times when he felt almost immune from detection,' said Bundy. 'At times, he felt that no matter how much he fucked up, nothing could go wrong.'

Once he had abducted Janice and Denise, he 'would not be able to drive a great distance without arousing the suspicions of the girls in the car. And so, he would seek a secluded space, a secluded area, within a fairly short driving distance of the Lake Sammamish area.'

They'd talk as he drove.

'But once the individual would have her in a spot where he had, you know, security over her, then there would be a minimum amount of conversation, which would be, you know, designed to avoid developing some kind of a relationship.'

Again, Bundy liked to distance himself from his crimes by pretending what he was saying was mere speculation.

'He had a house somewhere in the area, and took them there, one girl to the house and came back and got the other one. That's one hypothesis. The second hypothesis would be that he had killed the first girl and then returned sometime later to search out a second individual.'

He would then subdue the girl with the powerful weapon he had at his disposal.

'Fear. I suppose in such circumstances we could expect some sort of fear factor – a knife, a gun, anything to gain the attention of the individual...'

He was also indifferent about how he killed his victim.

'I don't know. Strangle her, stab her, something.'

Bundy was well aware of the risks of taking two victims from the same place on one day.

'In all likelihood, this person knew about the criminal investigation process,' he said.

Indeed, he did. During this period, Bundy was working as the Assistant Director of the Seattle Crime Prevention Advisory Commission, where he wrote a pamphlet for women on rape prevention. Then, he worked at the Department of Emergency Services, a state agency involved in the search for the missing women.

'If he had been acting more rationally, he would have realized that the disappearance of two girls in this fashion would yield a tremendous amount more interest and activity on the part of the police.'

So why did he do it?

'It's possible he felt the first one wasn't satisfactory... since the first one worked, I guess he'd figure a similar approach would also be successful.'

The second abduction would be a duplicate of the first.

'Had he been cautious, he would've probably killed the first individual before leaving to get the second girl. But in this instance, since we've agreed he wasn't acting cautiously, he hadn't killed the first girl when he abducted the second.'

He then raped the second girl in front of the first. This left him with two bound victims.

'By this time, his frenzied compulsive activity of that day has run its course. Then, he realized the jeopardy he was in… So, he'd kill the two girls, place them in his car, and take them to a secluded area and leave them… He would not linger or relish the killing, since it was only a means to an end, to avoid detection.'

After that, he would go home and sleep.

Random rampage

Bundy moved on to study law at the University of Utah in Salt Lake City. Crossing Idaho on the way, he raped, murdered and dismembered a hitchhiker. Then, he began a series of attacks in Utah.

On 11 October 1974, 21-year-old student Rhonda Stapley was waiting at a bus stop when Bundy offered her a lift to the university. Instead, he drove her to a remote picnic spot. With his face inches from hers, he said quietly, 'Do you know what? I am going to kill you.' He put his hands around her throat and started squeezing. He choked and raped her repeatedly for three hours before she made her escape, but she did not report the incident to the police.

On 8 November, he approached 18-year-old Carol DaRonch in a shopping mall, introducing himself as 'Officer Roseland' and said that someone had attempted to break into her car.

'Would you mind coming with me, so we can check to see if anything has been stolen?' he asked.

He then insisted that she accompany him to police headquarters to sign a complaint. He said he would drive her there. When they stopped in a side street, she tried to jump out, but he was too quick for her and clapped a handcuff on her right wrist.

Growing angry, he pulled a small black gun from his pocket. Holding it to her head, he said, 'If you don't stop screaming, I'm going to kill you. I'll blow your brains out.'

Nevertheless, she managed to escape. But he was not done for the night.

At a high-school performance of the musical *The Red Head* nearby, he abducted 17-year-old student, Debra Kent. On the eve of his execution, he admitted killing her. He also admitted travelling to

Ted Bundy in 1975 as he helps Carol Bartholomew with the dishes after a party. Bundy presented a charming figure to the outside world and hid his dark secrets well.

Pocatello, Idaho on 5 May 1975 after a series of murders in Colorado. The following day, he lured 12-year-old Lynette Culver to his hotel room, raped her, drowned her in the bathtub and dumped her body in the Snake River. Asked why, he said, 'It was madness... It was basically to do what was done.'

Running the stop signs

On 16 August 1975, Bundy was back in Utah when he was arrested.

'I really didn't know what was on my mind,' he said, 'or what I wanted to do. I was a little bit fucked up.'

He was out cruising the streets, stoned.

'All I wanted to do was get home,' he said. 'I started off and it was at that point I saw lights in my rear-view mirror. I turned and they turned and all of a sudden I didn't feel right. It didn't look right to me. I turned again and it turned and it was clear that the car was following me. I really had no idea why. And so, I was just going to try to get away from it. I was very nervous...

'I went through the red light and turned on to what was obviously a main drag. I looked in the mirror as the car was coming around the corner and then there was this bright red glow on the side. That's the first I saw of that red light.'

Bundy panicked and took off at speed, neglecting to turn his headlights on. Sergeant Bob Hayward of the Utah Highway Patrol followed him as he ran two stop signs. He was coincidently the brother of Captain Pete Hayward, who was heading the homicide investigation in Utah.

Unable to shake off the patrol car, Bundy threw the dope out of the window and pulled into a derelict gas station. Keeping his hand on his .38, Hayward approached. The first thing he noticed was that the passenger-side seat had been removed and lay on its side on the back seat. Asked about this later by Detective Steve Bodiford, Bundy said, 'Well, I can carry things easier that way.'

'You mean you can carry bodies easier that way?' said Bodiford.

'Well, let's just say I can carry cargo better that way.'

'That cargo you carried, was it sometimes – was it damaged?' asked Bodiford.

'Sometimes it was damaged and sometimes it wasn't,' said Bundy.

The evidence stacks up

Tools that could be used in burglary were also found in his car, along with a pair of handcuffs. His photograph was picked out by Carol DaRonch as the man who had tried to abduct her on the night Debra Kent went missing.

His credit card receipts showed that he filled up with petrol where women had gone missing in Colorado. A witness from the Wildwood Inn in Snowmass, Colorado, where 23-year-old registered nurse, Caryn Campbell, had gone missing on 12 January 1975 – her nude body was found on a dirt road just outside the resort a month later – recognized him from his mugshot.

When he phoned Liz Kendall, she told him she had had conversations with the police in Salt Lake City and King County, Washington.

'It's okay. You did what you had to do,' Bundy said. 'If you told them the truth, then no harm has been done because the truth is good enough. The truth will prove me innocent.'

On 2 October 1975, Bundy was charged with the kidnapping and attempted murder of Carol DaRonch. Even so, Bundy made bail. He told reporters that he had been treated well by his jailers.

'Once you get underneath their exterior,' Bundy said, 'they're all nice people.'

The trial was welcome, he told newsmen.

'I want to clear my name,' he said, 'I want it all out in the open. I want it aired.'

Later, he said, 'I was trying to project an image. I was feeling proud of myself. That's when I started to be pleased about fucking with the press. From then on, it was a lot of fun.'

On 1 December 1975, Bundy was spotted on the campus of the University of Washington. The following day, he had lunch with Ann Rule, a former police officer who had worked alongside him at Seattle's Suicide Hotline Crisis Center.

'He continued to toss away the Utah charges as if they were no more important than a slight misunderstanding,' said Rule. 'He was supremely confident that he would win in court in the DaRonch case.'

Finally, she asked him about the women who had gone missing in Washington state. He denied even reading about them in the paper. And when Rule asked Bundy, 'Do you like women?' he said, 'Yes, I think I do.'

In denial

At his trial in February 1976, Bundy waived his right to a jury and claimed he had an alibi. He said his car had broken down on the afternoon of 8 November 1974, and he pushed it into a gas station, where a mechanic helped him to start it. He drove home to his apartment around 5pm. Later on, Bundy remembered, he went out to try to start the car, but couldn't. He added, 'I'm not going to fool anybody, it's hard to think back 10 months, 12 months – 16 months now.'

He knew he was home by 11 that night because his telephone records showed he called Liz Kendall in Seattle. He had told her that his world was 'falling apart'.

He denied having been at the mall where Carol DaRonch said he had picked her up. Nor had he had any contact with DaRonch. As for the handcuffs found in his car, he said, 'In the early part of 1975, in the course of doing work for my landlord, I took things to the Salt Lake City dump, and I found them in a box of odds and ends there.'

'Did you ever have a key to those handcuffs?' asked prosecutor, David Yocom.

'I don't believe so.'

'Wouldn't be much value to you in apprehending people without a key, would there?'

'Well, again, if that was my purpose, as I say, the absence of a key was one of the primary factors in saying they were more of a curiosity than something one could use that would have any utility,' said Bundy.

'But you told [Colorado Detective Ben] Forbes you were going to use them to restrain people, is that right?'

Bundy demurred.

'Do you remember what you told the officers about the crowbar in the automobile?'

'I can't remember specifically,' said Bundy. 'I think I may have told them I had been using it that day, shortly before that day. I can't tell you exactly what I said that evening.'

'A crowbar of this nature is not exactly a tool that you would use with regard to repairing your automobile, is it?' said Yocom.

'Well, it's a useful tool. What can I say, Dave?'

This mock civility did not blunt Yocom's attack.

Yocom asked Bundy if he had purchased a total of 22.7 gallons of gas in a four-day period in late October, all within the Bountiful-Murray area where the attack on DaRonch had taken place.

'So, can you tell me generally in your head how many miles you travelled on 23 gallons of gas?'

'Oh, I'm not really thinking about it, Dave. I thought you made your own conclusion. I'm not here to do mathematical problems.'

'Didn't you brag to a woman acquaintance that you like virgins and you can have them at any time?' Yocom continued.

'No,' said Bundy.

'Didn't you tell that same woman that you saw no difference between right and wrong?'

'I don't remember that statement. If I made it, it was taken out of context and does not represent my views.'

Bundy was then caught out in a series of lies. They were small ones that might have been dismissed by a jury, but they damaged his plausibility as the judge pointed out in his summing up.

Fearing the worst, Bundy told Liz, 'If I can't be free, I want to be dead.'

Extradition order

He was found guilty of aggravated kidnap. When a guard tried to handcuff him, Bundy said, 'You don't need those. I'm not going anywhere.'

He put the verdict down to the fact that it had been reported he was about to be indicted for the murder of Caryn Campbell in Colorado.

'I would have ridden out the DaRonch thing,' Bundy said later, 'but a murder beef in Colorado was something different. Fuck that bullshit!'

'The Colorado trial will mark the beginning of the end of a myth,' he told Ann Rule in October 1976.

The extradition order came just before Christmas – 'My Christmas present from the court,' Bundy told a friend on the phone, 'a guaranteed death sentence.'

'I began seriously planning an escape,' he said. 'I knew absolutely nothing about the art of escaping. So, to acquire the necessary information, I began to talk at great length with prisoners I knew had themselves escaped prison in the past. I doubt that I learned anything, except that the fewer people you talk to about such things, the better.'

On 27 January 1977, he was transferred to Aspen in a four-door Ford sedan. Mike Fisher sat beside him.

'Someone in the car was wearing cologne,' Bundy recalled, 'the first cologne I'd smelled in months and months and months. I can remember a sudden surge of elation, of almost freedom. I probably hadn't felt so good since some time before I was first arrested. I said to myself, "I've got a chance now. There'll be a chance for something."'

And he was going to be ready.

'I got hold of an atlas which had maps of all the states, and I studied the area surrounding Aspen to the point where I thought I'd memorized all the roads, towns and highway distances,' he said. 'Based on a number of factors, I decided that it would be wisest to go toward a place called Crested Butte, then down to Gunnison, Colorado and south to Durango and then make my way east toward some large city on the east coast.'

On the loose

Bundy elected to conduct his own defence and was given permission to use the law library on the first floor of the Pitkin County Courthouse.

'Things,' he said, 'finally seemed to be coming together. I decided that I'd make the attempt on Tuesday, 7 June.'

He jumped from the window of the law library. But after six days, he was recaptured.

Returned to Garfield County Jail, Bundy made a second escape attempt. Gaining access to the crawl space above the ceiling took him to the head jailer's apartment, where he changed his clothes. Elated, he walked out into the snow.

This time, he made it all the way to Tallahassee.

He found himself near the campus of Florida State University. There, in the early hours of 15 January 1978, he broke into Chi Omega's sorority house, where two students, aged 20 and 21, were brutally murdered, and two other 21-year-olds survived with horrendous injuries. In a basement apartment in nearby Dunwoody Street, another 21-year-old woman suffered life-changing injuries.

Bundy then headed to Jacksonville, where he attempted to abduct a 14-year-old girl but was scared off by her older brother. Then, in

Lake City, he abducted, raped, murdered and mutilated a 12-year-old called Kimberly Leach. He was arrested near the Alabama state line, after a policeman fired two warning shots.

'I wish you had just killed me back there,' said Bundy. 'If I run now, will you shoot me?'

Liz Kendall called later and asked Bundy about the Florida murders.

'He told me that he didn't want to talk about them,' she told Detective Bob Keppel, 'but then… he said that he felt like he had a disease like alcoholism or something like alcoholics that couldn't take another drink, and he told me it was just something that he couldn't be around and he knew it now. And I asked what that was, and he said, "Don't make me say it."'

They talked about a phone call he had made to her from Salt Lake City late at night when Debra Kent had been abducted.

'I always thought, well, he couldn't be out abducting women because I'd talked to him on the phone that night,' she said, 'and I asked if he didn't sometimes call me or come over to touch base with reality after he'd done some of these things, and he said, "That's a pretty good guess."'

They spoke again two days later.

'He said he wanted to talk about what we'd been talking about in the first phone call. And I said, "You mean about being sick?" And he said, "Yes…" He told me that he was sick and was consumed by something he didn't understand, and that, ah, that he just couldn't contain it.'

Keppel asked Liz why Bundy couldn't control himself.

'Well, he said that he tried, he said that it took so much of his time, and that's why he wasn't doing well in law school; and that he couldn't seem to get his act together, because he spent so much time trying to maintain a normal life and he just couldn't do it. He said that he was preoccupied with this force… He mentioned an incident about following a sorority girl. He didn't do anything that night, but he just told me that's how it was, that he was out late at night and he would follow people like that, but that he'd try not to, but he just did it anyway…'

The Washington murders came up in conversation.

'He did talk about Lake Sammamish, he started by saying that he was sick, and he said, "I don't have a split personality, and I don't have blackouts." He said, "I remember everything that I've done." And he mentioned the day, 14 July, when two women were abducted from Lake Sammamish and we went out to eat around five and he was saying that he remembered that he ate two hamburgers and enjoyed every bite. And that we went to Ferrell's and he said that it wasn't that he had forgotten what he'd done that day or that he couldn't remember, but just said that it was over.'

Cold-hearted son of a bitch

During interviews, Detective Bodiford said Bundy was sometimes almost amenable, admitting to a taste for voyeurism and pornography.

'I want you to understand me, so you can understand my problem,' he said, adding that he never enjoyed what he did, but had to do it to keep his fantasies alive. 'The act was a downer. What was the act? I'm not going to tell you the modus operandi.'

He also said, 'Sometimes I feel like a vampire,' insisting, 'I never hurt anyone I knew.'

Talking of a girl he had seen when out cycling, he said, 'I had to have her at any cost.' Nothing more.

Bundy also told Bodiford, 'I'm the most cold-hearted son of a bitch you'll ever meet.'

On the other hand, he said, 'I like to go out and have a good time like anyone else. I'm not a bad guy! I like to have a few drinks.'

As well as Liz, he kept in contact with old girlfriend, Carole Boone, a twice-divorced mother of two.

'I've got a lot of friends that stick with me through thick and thin,' he said.

In a letter to Carole, he dismissed the FBI as 'Fornicators, Bastards and Imposters'.

'I love you, Boone,' he wrote. 'I need you. More than ever.'

He addressed her as 'Darling Boone', 'Tender Peachblossom', 'Precious Fleshpot' and 'My Beloved Quintessential Quark'.

With detectives, Bundy hinted that he might be persuaded to make a full confession if he could be transferred to a prison in Washington state.

'I'm interested in clearing everything up,' said Bundy. 'It requires talking to... starting with somebody in Seattle, and to make some inquiries, and it requires talking to somebody in Utah.'

He said he wanted 'everybody being satisfied... to get all the answers they want to all the questions they want to ask, then after that was all over, I would like to go back to Washington state. That's where my mother is, that's where my family is, and that's where I'm from... Washington has a lot of questions to ask me.'

But if he was extradited back to Washington state to stand trial, he would then have to be returned to Florida to face charges there.

'I'm not talking about trials,' said Bundy. 'There would be no need for trials,' he said, indicating that he would not contest the charges. The idea was 'giving knowledge and peace of mind that can be returned to people who don't know what happened to their loved ones'.

The truth about Bundy

While playing to the camera at press conferences, he wrote to *The New York Times* complaining about the articles written about him.

'I have never had the opportunity to address myself fully to all the accusations, inferences, innuendo, rumours and suspicion ad nauseam,' he said. 'What has irked me about the stories written on my case is that anyone with a badge or a bachelor of arts degree is considered an expert on Theodore Bundy and what makes him tick. Prosecutors, policemen, journalists, old girlfriends, friends and family of the "victims", psychologists, psychiatrists, ex-roommates, former teachers and defence attorneys have all ventured opinions, observations and assorted drivel about this mysterious creature. I think it's my turn now. I am, after all, the ultimate Bundy expert.'

In the face of an expert assessment of his mental condition, Bundy dismissed any attempt to understand him on the psychological level. And when the public defender sought to make a plea bargain, Bundy refused, saying, 'I felt like he was conceding that I was guilty. And if you look at the cases he takes, that's essentially what he does, just avoids the death penalty. I didn't consider myself in that category.'

Prima donna in the dock

When the trial for the Tallahassee sorority house rampage began, Bundy complained that he was not ready.

'We will begin, Mr Bundy,' Judge Edward Cowart insisted.

'Then you'll start without me, Your Honour,' Bundy said.

Bundy then employed delaying tactics and was found in contempt of court.

'I'm willing to accept the consequences of my actions, Your Honour,' said Bundy.

'Then we're together,' said Judge Cowart. 'I just hope you stay with us. If you don't, we'll miss you.'

Looking round the crowded courtroom, Bundy said, 'And all these people won't pay their money to come and see me.'

Bundy insisted on discharging his attorneys and conducting his own defence. But when Judge Cowart refused to let him contest the forensic evidence, Bundy mumbled some derogatory statements under his breath.

'You impress me not, sir,' the judge admonished.

'Well, I suppose the feeling is mutual, Your Honour,' Bundy replied.

Convicted of two counts of murder and five other felony counts, Bundy got his chance to address the court.

'I'm not asking for mercy,' he said. 'For I find it somewhat absurd to ask for mercy for something I did not do... I believe if I'd been able to develop fully the evidence – which supports my innocence, which indeed I think created a reasonable doubt – and been able to have quality representation, I'm confident that I would have been acquitted, and, in the event I get a new trial, will be acquitted.

'It wasn't easy sitting through this trial for a number of reasons. But the main reason it was not easy in the early part of the case was the presentation of the state's case on what took place in the Chi Omega House, the blood, the pictures, the bloodstained sheets. And to note the state was trying to find me responsible was not easy. And it was not easy, nor did I ignore the families of these young women. I do not know them. And I do not think it's hypocritical of me, God knows, to say I sympathize with them, the best I can. Nothing like this has ever happened to anyone close to me.

'But I'm telling the court, and I'm telling those people close to the victims in this case: I'm not the one responsible for the acts in the Chi Omega House or Dunwoody Street... As a consequence, I cannot accept the sentence even though one will be imposed and even though I realize the lawful way the court will impose it – because it is not a sentence on me; it is a sentence on someone else who is not standing here today. So, I will be tortured for and receive the pain for that act... but I will not share the burden or the guilt.'

Bundy relished the drama being played out.

'And now the burden is on this court,' he said. 'And I don't envy you. The court is like a hydra right now. It's been asked to dispense no mercy as the maniac at the Chi Omega House dispensed no mercy. It's asked to consider this case as a man and a judge. And you're asked also to render the wisdom of a god. It's like some incredible Greek tragedy.

Ted Bundy reacts to the guilty verdict in court.

It must have been written sometime and it must be one of those ancient Greek plays that portrays the three faces of man.'

Judge Cowart was unmoved and Bundy was sentenced to death.

When the trial for the murder of 12-year-old Kimberly Leach in Lake City began, Bundy also conceded that he would probably be convicted again, protesting that the odds were stacked against him and refused to accept the jury.

'I'm leaving,' Bundy said, attempting to stalk out of the courtroom. 'This is a game and I won't be a party to it! I'm not staying in this kind of Waterloo.'

Then he yelled at the prosecutor, 'You want a circus? I'll make a circus. I'll rain on your parade, Jack. You'll see a thunderstorm.'

He headed for the door, but the bailiff blocked his path.

After his outburst in court, he told Carole, 'I'm coming unglued. I just can't keep it together anymore… witness after witness Lie! Lie! Lie! Lie!'

Crazy marriage proposal

Calling Carole as a character witness, Bundy seized the opportunity to ask her to marry him. She said yes. As this was sworn in front of a judge, Bundy declared that they were legally married.

When the jury returned with a guilty verdict, Bundy jumped to his feet and shouted at the judge, 'Tell the jury they were wrong!'

Awaiting sentencing, Bundy said, 'The one thing I like about this is that at least there's no suspense.'

Special Agent Bill Hagmaier of the FBI's Behavioral Science Unit visited Bundy and asked about the victims who were found with fresh make-up and newly washed hair. Bundy said, 'If you've got time, they can be anything you want them to be.'

He also admitted to taking Polaroid pictures of them as souvenirs, explaining, 'When you work hard to do something right, you don't want to forget it.'

He told Hagmaier that the murders were not about lust or violence, but possession.

'They are part of you,' Bundy said. 'After a while, when you plan these, that person becomes a part of you and you are forever one... Even after 20 or 30, it's the same thing because you are the last one there. You feel the last bit of breath leaving their body. You're looking into their eyes and, basically, a person in that situation is God. You then possess them and they shall forever be part of you. And the grounds where you kill them or leave them become sacred to you, and you will always be drawn back to them.'

Other visitors were told, 'I don't know why everyone is out to get me.'

'He really and truly did not have a sense of what he had done,' said Dr Lewis, the defence psychiatrist who examined him in prison.

While in jail, Bundy was interviewed by journalists Stephen G Michaud and Hugh Aynesworth for their book, *The Only Living Witness*, which the New York *Daily News* called 'one of the ten best crime books ever written'.

'I don't care what you write,' Bundy said, 'just so you get it right, and just so it sells.'

'Just a dream'

Asked about the victims, Bundy said they 'just fit the general criteria of being young and attractive'.

Would certain women attract an assailant by the way they move or act?

'What we're talking about here is just opportunity,' he said, 'as opposed to more discreet factors that would be exhibited by the person.'

He posited the situation where he was driving one evening and saw an attractive teenager walking down the street.

'Because the area was dark and she was alone, he decided to select her as the victim for this intended act of sexual assault. He parked his car down the street and then ran up behind the girl… As he came up behind her, she heard him. She turned around and he brandished a knife and grabbed her by the arm and told her to do what he wanted her to do…

'He pushed her off the sidewalk into this darkened wooded area and told her to submit and do what he wanted her to do. She began to argue with him and he kept telling her to be quiet… Then he began to try to remove her clothes and she would continue to struggle in a feeble manner. And also to voice verbally her objections to what was going on. And then the significance now is that his intent with this victim was not to harm her…

'But he found himself with this girl who was struggling and screaming… There were houses in the vicinity, and he was concerned that somebody might hear. And so, in an attempt to stop her from talking or arguing, he placed his hand over her mouth…

'Let's say he placed his hands around her throat just to throttle her into unconsciousness, so that she wouldn't scream anymore. She stopped struggling and it appeared she was unconscious. But not, in his opinion, to the point where he had killed her.

'Then let's say he removed her clothes and raped her and put his own clothes back on. At about that point, he began to notice that the girl wasn't moving… And then, in a fit of panic, he fled the scene.

'He got back into his car and drove back to his house, still not knowing if the girl was alive or dead. But once he returned to the house, upon reflection he began to wonder… So he decided to return to the scene and if the body was there to recover it and take it somewhere else where it wouldn't be found…'

This was the fate of 16-year-old cheerleader, Nancy Wilcox, who disappeared from Holladay, Utah, on the outskirts of Salt Lake City on 2 October 1974. Initially, the police thought she was a runaway. Her body was never found.

Aynesworth wondered if talking about what he had done would remove a burden from Bundy's mind.

'A burden? I carry no burden, except being in prison,' he said. 'I've learned to live absolutely and completely and totally in the here and now. I don't worry, think, or concern myself with the past or, for that matter, with the future, except only to the extent necessary... Whatever I've done in the past, you know – the emotions of omissions or commissions – doesn't bother me. It's not real. It's just a dream.'

He felt no guilt.

'Guilt. It's this mechanism we use to control people. It's an illusion. It's a kind of social control mechanism and it's very unhealthy. It does terrible things to our bodies. I'm in the enviable position of not having to deal with guilt. There's just no reason for it. I don't think I need to feel guilty anymore...'

Crocodile tears

With five days to go before his execution, Bundy did eventually confess to Bill Hagmaier and Bob Keppel, promising to provide every detail.

'I'm not asking for clemency,' he said. 'I'm not asking to get off. I'm not asking for sympathy. But I draw the line. We need a period of time. Sixty, ninety days. A few months. Systematically going over it with everybody. Bottom to top. Everything I can think of. Get it all down... I'll give you something substantial right now. To show you that my head is in the right place. A couple of months is not going to make any difference.'

Then in his last interview, Dobson said that Bundy wept. 'He expressed great regret, remorse for what he had done, for the families that were hurting.'

The law then took its course. As Bundy was strapped into the electric chair, he addressed his last remarks to his lawyer, Jim Coleman, and Methodist minister, Fred Lawrence.

'Jim and Fred,' he said. 'I'd like you to give my love to my family and friends.'

CHAPTER TWO

Jeffrey Dahmer

'Milwaukee Cannibal' Jeffrey Dahmer killed and dismembered 17 male partners between 1978 and 1991. His later murders involved cannibalism and necrophilia, sometimes chemically preserving victims' bodies for later sexual use. He even experimented with zombifying victims, so that he would have a passive sexual partner constantly available.

Dahmer was arrested on 22 July 1991 when 32-year-old Tracy Edwards flagged down a patrol car on the corner of North 25th Street. He asked the officers to unlock the handcuffs on his wrists. Their key did not fit, so they accompanied Edwards back to the apartment where he said he had been cuffed.

The flat belonged to Jeffrey Dahmer. Edwards told the officers that Dahmer had threatened him with a large knife. They found the knife, along with Polaroid pictures of male bodies in various stages of dismemberment and the head of a young black man in the fridge. At the police station on North Vel R. Phillips Avenue, Dahmer was interviewed by Detective Patrick Kennedy. He was understandably depressed.

'What am I going to do?' Dahmer groaned. 'It wasn't supposed to end like this! No, no, I can't do this. Pat, please take your gun out and kill me. I want to die. I had it all planned out. I'm not supposed to be here. I should have done it a long time ago and saved myself all of this. It's over anyways. Please, Pat, take your gun out and shoot me, just end it!'

Hydrochloric acid had been found in Dahmer's apartment.

'Do you know what hydrochloric acid would do to you if you put it into your veins?' he said. 'Just inject some hydrochloric acid or formaldehyde into your veins by using a hypodermic needle. The acid would travel right to your heart and boom – it would be all over, no pain, no problem. I should have done it. I wanted to so many times.'

Kennedy took off his gun and locked it in his desk drawer, assuring Dahmer that he was not going to kill him.

'For what I've done, I should be killed,' said Dahmer. 'I know they will never let me out again… I can't believe I was so stupid! I never thought I'd get caught like this! I was always so careful. I guess I just got drunk.'

He did not want his family to be informed of his arrest.

'Look, what I did, I did alone,' he said. 'I don't want them to know what I've done. I don't want them involved in this thing in any way!'

There had been news cameras outside his block when he had been arrested, so his family were going to find out anyway.

'Oh my God! What will they think of me when they find out? Pat, I beg you, go get your gun and end this thing for me right now! I can't take this, please!'

Kennedy's colleagues who were searching his apartment were a bit wary of what they might find.

'Go ahead and search,' said Dahmer. 'You're going to find out everything anyway. Don't worry, nothing will explode. It's just some chemicals; it won't hurt anybody as long as it stays in the boxes.'

Kennedy tried his best to be friendly and reassuring.

'Pat, when you find out what I've done, you'll hate me,' Dahmer said. 'Everyone will… You haven't seen the things I've done. How will I ever be able to live with myself, or face my family again?'

Dahmer was surprised by the easy time he was getting.

'You know, Pat, this is nothing like I thought it would be,' he said. 'I guess I just never imagined that my interrogation would be like this. You're going to find out everything now anyways, so I might as well tell you everything, but if I'm going to tell you, I should start at the beginning.'

Sex fantasies

Kennedy was expecting Dahmer to tell him about the head in the refrigerator. Instead, he started talking about an incident that had occurred in his hometown of Bath, Ohio 13 years earlier when he was 18.

At the time, his parents were going through a messy divorce and he was left alone in the family home.

'I didn't like sleeping alone in that big house,' he said. 'It made me angry. I started to have fleeting fantasies of killing someone. I don't know where they came from, but they did. They were always intertwined, sex and killing. I tried to get them out of my mind, but the sexual fantasy was powerful and I masturbated for hours thinking about it. The fantasy was always the same. I met a good-looking man, brought him home, had sex with him and then killed him. In my fantasy, I always strangled them as they slept.'

Dahmer knew early on that he was gay – which was unacceptable as he was a Lutheran.

'I don't know why, but my fantasies always included cutting into the dead bodies of my lovers. I sliced their torso from chin to crotch and pulled out their inner viscera, laying it on their chest. The thought of the warm inner cavity excited me tremendously, and I masturbated thinking about it.'

He told his dad that he was fascinated by the inner workings of small creatures and that he wanted to preserve their bones for future study. His dad, a chemist, taught him how to use chemicals to remove the dead skin.

'My sexual interests and cutting up dead animals slowly merged,' he said. 'The two thoughts became one, and I couldn't think about sex with a man without also having thoughts of cutting open his human body and examining the insides.'

Rotting flesh

One day, he picked up a hitchhiker and invited the young man home. They got drunk and started kissing. When the young man wanted to leave, Dahmer tried to prevent him. There was a fight and Dahmer hit him with a barbell and killed him.

He dragged the body out to a wooded area behind the house and hid it in the brush. Checking on the body every so often, he noticed the flesh had rotted away or been eaten by animals. Then he got a sledgehammer, smashed up the skeleton and scattered the shards of bones.

After a row with his father, Dahmer quit college and spent two years in the Army. Unable to settle back home because of his heavy drinking, he went to live with his grandmother in a large house in the West Allis suburb of Milwaukee in December 1981. She was religious and he went to church with her. Bible study kept him sober during the days. But once she had gone to bed, he was plagued with fantasies of having sex with men, who he would dominate, kill and dismember.

Dahmer was in a local library when a young man dropped a note on his desk that read, 'If you want a blow job meet me in the men's room, five minutes.' The guy wasn't there, but this was a turning point.

'This is when I decided to give in to the dark side,' he said. 'Grandma's way was not working. I was miserable and lonely, so I decided to indulge my sexual lusts and fantasies.'

He began hanging out in gay bars, often bringing back his pick-ups for sex in his grandmother's basement or hotels downtown. One night, he picked up a guy in a transgender hangout.

'This is the truth, Pat. I really don't know what happened,' said Dahmer. 'The last thing I remember, we were lying naked in bed. I must have blacked out because, when I came to the next morning, the guy was dead. My hands and arms were sore and bruised, and his face and chest were black, blue and bloody. It looked as though he had taken a terrible beating. I swear, Pat, I don't remember what I did, but I figure I must have beaten him to death in a drunken rage when he tried to leave. I quickly got up and cleaned myself off, trying to figure out what to do with the dead guy.'

Man in a suitcase

It was the morning of Thanksgiving and he had to get back to his grandmother's for dinner as his father, stepmother and younger brother were all in town for the holiday.

A mugshot of Jeffrey Dahmer from 1991.

'I remember calling a cab and had him take me to the Grand Avenue Mall. It was open until noon that day. At a department store, I bought the biggest suitcase I could find. It was the kind that had the side zipper feature, making it easy to fill with large items. It came equipped with little rollers on the bottom. I took the cab back to the hotel and told the driver to wait. I went up to my room and carefully folded my dead roommate and all his belongings into the suitcase. I know it sounds strange, but the guy folded right into the thing, just like it was designed for him. The cab driver helped me carry everything out to the car and placed the suitcase into the trunk. Then he drove me to Grandma's house.'

Dahmer took the suitcase down to the basement and left it there while he enjoyed Thanksgiving dinner.

'It was strange,' he said, 'but I wasn't even nervous. Nobody had the slightest idea what was going on.'

Next day, when everyone was out, he cut up the body over the drain in the basement, masturbating several times as he did so. He double-wrapped the chunks of flesh in garbage bags, then smashed up the skeleton with a sledgehammer. Everything went into a large dumpster behind the garage, while he poured bleach down the drain.

'The garbage men came and took all the evidence away: nothing was ever said, no one ever knew,' he said. 'I had gotten away with murder for the second time.'

No remorse

He continued picking up men in gay bars and bringing them back to his grandmother's house for sex.

'It was easy and exciting,' he said, 'but when they left in the middle of the night, I always felt empty and alone. I hated that.'

He had got away with two murders and decided to kill again.

'I felt it was stupid to try to control my desires,' he said. 'It seemed as if life conspired to allow my lusts. The situation just kept presenting itself. More importantly, there were no consequences. All I know is, after that, I had to disconnect with my conscience. I no longer felt any sense of remorse.'

This time, he got some sleeping pills to knock out his victims.

'Most men that I have been with want to have anal sex with me,' he explained. 'I enjoy all the touching and kissing. I love giving and getting oral sex, but anal sex is uncomfortable and hurts. I know it sounds selfish, but I thought if I could render them unconscious, I could spend hours pleasuring myself and not have to reciprocate.'

Two months later, he drugged a young Hispanic man he had brought home. He was delighted to discover that, despite being unconscious, his partner could still get an erection.

When Dahmer woke in the morning, he was afraid that the man might tell the police that he had been drugged, so he strangled the young man while he was still unconscious.

'I remember that, after I strangled him, I had anal sex with him and felt that it was a shame that it was all over so soon. I wrapped him in a sheet and laid him in the fruit cellar. I returned several times throughout the week to kiss, rub and have anal sex with him. When he began to rot, I severed the flesh from his body with a knife, double-wrapped it in garbage bags and threw them in the trash. I wrapped the skeleton in a sheet and used a sledgehammer from Grandma's garage to smash the bones and dispose of them in the same way. I kept his head. He was real nice-looking and I wanted to keep part of him.'

All this was done one Sunday before his grandmother got back from church.

'I almost couldn't believe what I did, yet just thinking about it gave me great pleasure.'

While he constantly checked the newspapers and TV news bulletins, there was no mention of any of his victims. He began to feel that he was untouchable.

Kennedy could scarcely believe what he was hearing, but his colleagues who were searching Dahmer's apartment had found four skulls, several frozen heads and there were human bones all over the place. Clearly, Dahmer was telling the truth.

Dahmer would have to make amends for what he had done if he was ever to find peace of mind, Kennedy had said.

'How will I ever be able to make amends for what I did?' Dahmer asked. 'I mean, I don't even know the names of these guys, and who should I make amends to?'

Kennedy pointed out that, if they could identify his victims, at least their families would know what had happened to them.

'I think you have something, Pat,' Dahmer said. 'It's the least I can do, maybe the only thing I can do.'

He would tell all.

Murder in mind

Next, Dahmer said he had picked up a young mixed-race guy about a month after the last murder. Following a night of sex with his unconscious body, he strangled him and disposed of the body as before, but he was beginning to have misgivings.

'I was mixed up about the whole thing,' Dahmer confessed. 'I loved having these guys with me and making love to them. Their warm bodies were under my complete control. But after killing them, I felt empty, and the task of disposing of their bodies was no easy job. When it was done, I felt empty and alone.'

For a while, he played it straight, but when his lovers left in the morning, he still felt that terrible loneliness.

'No one really wanted a relationship,' he complained. 'Just quick, anonymous sex and that's it. It was over in an instant and they were gone. I struggled with these feelings for about a year and felt lucky that I had not been found out. I continued to cruise the gay bars, picking up guys to have sex with, but it was shallow and unfulfilling.'

He lived in hope of finding someone who would fall in love with him, but it didn't happen. Worse, he kept thinking of his dead lovers, remembering the control over them while he masturbated.

'I knew I was lucky to go undetected and I was afraid my luck would run out,' he said. 'I feared that I would be caught, but the allure of a warm body, one that would not leave at the end of the night, stayed with me, and I constantly thought about killing again.'

Nude Polaroids

His next victim was a young Mexican who chatted him up at a bus stop. Dahmer took him home, drugged him, killed him and put his dismembered body out with the trash.

The fear of being found out excited him, but to have a free hand he needed to find a place of his own, so he rented a one-bedroom apartment not far from the chocolate factory where he worked. He brought guys back there for sex without killing them.

'One day as I sat and drank, I saw this young Asian male,' he said. 'He was a little younger than I would have liked, but he was eager and willing. I offered him 50 bucks to come home with me and let me take some nude photographs of him. We drank some rum and Cokes and I took some Polaroids, but he was very young and not that developed sexually, so I didn't kill him.'

This time, Dahmer found he was sailing a little too close to the wind.

'He must have told his parents,' he said, 'because about two hours after he left, the police were at my door, found the photos I took, and arrested me. I thought this was it, that everything would come out, but the cops were only interested in the photos I took of the Asian kid and nothing else. I remember that my father was upset when I called from jail, but he got me a lawyer. I made a plea arrangement in court and was put on work release for about a year.'

Having to report to the authorities every night after work curtailed his activities, but, after the year was up, he began hanging around gay bars again. Soon after, he met a black guy in front of a porno bookstore.

'This guy was big, strong, and well built. He said he was a player and I asked him if he would come home with me,' Dahmer said. 'I told him I would give him 50 bucks if he let me perform oral sex on him and take some nude photos. I don't think he was gay, but he was really nice-looking and his body was lean and attractive. One of the best-looking guys that I had ever met...

'When we got back to my apartment, he took off his clothes and I began to go down on him, but he made it clear that he wasn't a fag and said that, if I didn't pay him the money I offered, he would kick my ass and take everything I had.'

Dahmer was not afraid because he had already spiked his drink.

'I knew that within minutes he would be mine. After he fell asleep, I made love to him for hours. I enjoyed him so much that I kept him alive a little longer than usual. In the morning, I could tell by his breathing that he was coming out of his drug-induced state, so I began to strangle him. But the drug had worn off and as I choked him, he began to struggle with me. I panicked, realizing that I was not strong enough to overcome him, so I grabbed a knife and stabbed him in the carotid artery.'

This is a main artery that carries blood to the brain, Dahmer explained.

After that, he took a number of nude photographs of his victim in various positions. The police found a photograph of the man with an incision from his chin to his genitals. His entrails had been pulled out and laid out on top of his torso.

'I wanted a picture of his insides, so I placed him in the bathroom and cut him open,' said Dahmer. 'I pulled the viscera from his body with my hands. The look and feel of it gave me unbelievable pleasure, and I masturbated and made love to him by placing my penis in it, like having intercourse.'

Getting rid of the evidence

He was always naked during dismemberment, so he would not get blood on his clothes. Meanwhile, he would slug on Budweiser.

Once he was satisfied, he cut up the body in the bathtub with a knife he had bought for the purpose. Severed heads, hands and genitals were placed in the kitchen sink to keep them fresh and lifelike. He usually kept the genitals preserved in formaldehyde and air-dried on a towel for future oral sex. Then, he flushed the severed flesh down the lavatory or put it in trash bags to be left out for the garbage collection.

Cutting the tendons and cartilage, he pulled the bones apart and put them in a large plastic garbage pail he'd bought. Then he poured in hydrochloric acid to dissolve them. After a few days, the resulting sludge was flushed down the toilet.

'I knew now that I was in it till the end, and this one was so sexually satisfying that I began to feel remorse that it was over so soon,' Dahmer said. 'It seemed a shame to get rid of the whole body, so I decided to keep his head.'

Asked about the other skulls that had been found, Dahmer said: 'I wanted to keep those guys with me. But after a while, they gave off an awful smell. As a matter of fact, the smell was a problem that I constantly had to deal with, so I bought a large, ten-gallon soup kettle at the mall and began boiling the heads in a solution of hot water and cleansing soaps. After being in the solution for about an hour, the hair and flesh just boiled right off and left the skull. I kept the finished ones in my closet. Any clothing, jewellery, identification or other property of the guys that I brought home, I cut up and threw out.'

The slurry from boiling the heads was flushed down the toilet, while the brain tissue was dug out with a large serving spoon. He explained that, if you severed the head in the right place at the base of the neck, you could fit the spoon in and scrape out the brain matter like cleaning out a pumpkin.

However, in the case of this good-looking guy, he made an exception.

'I decided to keep all of him,' he said. 'I filleted his flesh, muscles and tendons, and then boiled his whole skeleton.'

Expert butcher

Asked how he fitted a whole body into a ten-gallon kettle, Dahmer said, 'It's not hard if you know what you're doing. If you cut the joints properly, slicing the cartilage and tendons, the bones come right apart. After boiling and drying all the parts, I could place the entire body back together if I wanted to, and I did on occasion. Sometimes, after putting him back together on the floor of my apartment, I relived mentally what happened with him. I fantasized the whole scenario and got really turned on, and masturbated as I fondled his bones.'

He kept other parts that he preserved in acetone.

'When they were dried, I wore his scalp,' he said. 'It helped me to fantasize and remember the night I was with him. I could suck on his penis and masturbate.'

Three of the skulls looked different from the rest.

'They were some of the first ones I decided to keep,' Dahmer said. 'I wanted to keep part of them and decided on the skulls, but I was afraid someone might see them and detect what I was doing, so I bought some spray paint, a kind of fake granite colour, and painted them to look like fakes. I wanted the skulls to look like Halloween decorations. One I did in grey, one in green, and the other in a kind of brown-beige colour. Those were the only shades available, so I thought I would try each one. I did those when I was living at my grandma's because I feared that she might accidentally stumble on them while I was out of the house. After I got my own apartment, I had a security system, so I no longer had to paint the skulls anymore.'

Then, there were all the cleaning products found in the flat. It wasn't to clean up the blood as the police conjectured. He cut up the bodies in the bathtub, then let gravity do its job of carrying the blood down the drain. He had dissection down to a science. The cleaning products were to get rid of the smell.

'That was a constant problem for me,' he said. 'The smell was awful. I tried to keep the bodies with me for as long as I could after I killed them, but after a day or so they started to rot, depending on the temperature of my room. Summers were really the worst because I didn't have air-conditioning. When you fillet the flesh from the body, it gives off a horrendous odour. Several times the neighbours complained of the smell, so I constantly had air fresheners around. I even kept a fan going, using it as an exhaust for the fumes, pointing it out the bedroom window.'

Enough is never enough

After five victims, Dahmer said he thought it was time to stop.

'I thought that this would be enough to satisfy me, and that maybe I wouldn't have to kill again. But after about a month or so, the urge to have another warm, live human being under my complete control returned. It consumed me, and soon I was out looking to kill again.'

About a month after the first one, another black man he'd picked up went the same way. A month after that, he picked up another black guy in a gay club called La Cage and took him home. This time, Dahmer was out of sleeping pills.

'So, we drank into the early morning hours until the guy passed out,' he said. 'I just lay with him for a while listening to his heart, feeling his chest rise and fall. Then I had oral and anal sex with him and decided to kill him, so I strangled him. I remember I didn't keep any part of that guy. He wasn't that good-looking and I had time constraints.'

Garbage collections were on Monday morning, so, if Dahmer killed someone on a Friday night, he would have sex with the dead body until Sunday evening, then cut it up, putting the flesh in the garbage and dissolving the bones in acid.

Dahmer said he almost got caught with the next guy.

'I met this really nice-looking Asian guy one afternoon while I was at the mall downtown,' he said. 'I like going to the mall. There are always so many different types of people, all races and ethnic backgrounds, every size and shape.'

Dahmer was getting his knife sharpened in the cutlery shop.

'He was alone and really nice-looking, so I struck up a conversation with him. Well, I offered him 50 bucks to come home with me and let me take some photos. I told him that there was liquor at my place and indicated that I was sexually attracted to him. He was eager and co-operative, so we took the bus to my apartment. Once there, I gave him some money and he posed for several photos.'

Dahmer offered him a rum and Coke laced with sleeping pills.

'He drank it down quickly. We continued to drink until he passed out, and then I made love to him for the rest of the afternoon and early evening. I must have fallen asleep, because when I woke up it was late. I checked on the guy. He was out cold.'

Naked man in the street

He was out of beer, so Dahmer walked around the corner for another six-pack. But then he got drinking in the tavern and, before he knew it, it was closing time.

'I grabbed my six-pack and began walking home. As I neared my apartment, I noted a lot of commotion, people milling about, police officers and a fire engine. I decided to see what was going on, so I came closer. I was surprised to see they were all standing around the Asian guy from my apartment. He was standing there naked, speaking in some kind of Asian dialect.'

Jeffrey Dahmer in court. He was charged with 17 murders carried out between 1978 and 1991.

Dahmer panicked and walked on by, but he could see that the Asian boy was so messed up on booze and sleeping pills that he didn't know who or where he was.

'I don't really know why, but I strode into the middle of everyone and announced he was my lover. I said that we lived together at Oxford [apartments] and had been drinking heavily all day, and added that this was not the first time he left the apartment naked while intoxicated. I explained that I had gone out to buy some more beer and showed them the six-pack. I asked them to give him a break and let me take him back home.'

The firemen seemed to buy the story and drove off, but the police began to ask more questions and insisted that he take them to his apartment to discuss the matter further.

'I was nervous but felt confident; besides, I had no other choice,' said Dahmer.

One cop took the man by the arm and he followed, almost zombie-like.

'I led them to my apartment and once inside, I showed them the photos I had taken, and his clothes neatly folded on the arm of my couch. The cops kept trying to question the guy, but he was still talking gibberish and could not answer any of their questions, so I told them his name was Chuck Moung and gave them a phony date of birth.'

Dahmer gave them his ID and they wrote everything down in their notebooks.

'They seemed perturbed and talked about writing us some tickets for disorderly conduct or something. One of them said they should take us both in for all the trouble we had given them.'

As the police officers were discussing what to do, another call came over the radio. They left, letting Dahmer off with a warning and advising him to keep his drunken partner indoors.

'I was relieved. I had fooled the authorities and it gave me a tremendous feeling. I felt powerful, in control, almost invincible,' he said.

After the officers had gone, Dahmer gave his victim another sedative-laced drink and he soon passed out.

'I was still nervous about the narrow escape with the cops, so I strangled him and disposed of his body,' Dahmer said.

Please don't go

About a month after this incident, he took a Greyhound bus to Boystown, the gay district of Chicago, after there were complaints about him drugging patrons of gay bars in Milwaukee. In Chicago, he met a mixed-race guy who was Jewish and Puerto Rican. It was a Friday night and Dahmer persuaded him to come back with him to Milwaukee.

'I'm not particularly fond of receiving anal sex. It can be painful, but this guy was so willing and eager that I let him have his way.'

Dahmer did not even have to pay him.

'We spent the whole weekend together, almost like a real relationship,' Dahmer said. 'We made love and went to the mall, shopped for food to make dinner and everything. For a while, I thought that maybe this one would stay.'

But when Sunday night came, the man said he had a job in Chicago and would have to leave to get to work in the morning, so Dahmer drugged him.

'After he passed out, I had oral and anal sex with him and killed him, just like the others,' he said. 'I really didn't want to kill this one, but I had to because he was going to leave and I wanted to keep him with me. I took these Polaroids of him, placed his head in the freezer and… threw the flesh into the trash.'

A week or so later, he chatted up another guy at a bus stop and offered him 50 bucks to come back to his place for sex and drinks. He accepted and they took the bus to Dahmer's apartment. Once there, he gave him a spiked drink. After he passed out, Dahmer had sex with him and disposed of the body in the usual way.

At last, Dahmer got round to the head in the fridge.

'I met him a few days before my arrest. That's why he looked so fresh,' he said.

Dahmer kept his victims' heads in the refrigerator to preserve them for as long as they appeared lifelike.

'He was extremely handsome, the nicest-looking man I had ever met,' he said. 'I think he was a model or something, because he showed me some pictures of himself in professional poses. He was smooth-skinned and muscular, and more than willing to come home with me for cocktails and sex.

'I took my time with this one. Just looking at him gave me great pleasure. I hated to kill him and tried to keep as much of him as possible. I even kept his ID. You'll find it in my bedroom drawer.'

Knock at the door

Then, finally, there was the victim who had escaped and this led to Dahmer's arrest. Again, Dahmer was out of sleeping pills.

'But I still wanted to be with someone warm and alive,' he said. 'I went to the mall downtown and started drinking at a pub on the third floor. I met the guy there. We had a few beers together and talked. I figured that he was a willing prospect, so I offered him 50 bucks to come back to my apartment and let me take some pictures of him in the nude. He agreed.'

And Dahmer had a plan.

'I figured I'd ply him with booze until he passed out and then I would kill him, but this guy could really drink. I was getting drunk and knew that, if I wanted him, I would have to try something else. I asked him to let me take some bondage pictures of him, thinking that if I could handcuff him behind his back, he would be mine. Then I could knock him out by hitting him over the head or something, I don't know.'

But it went awry.

'I was drunk and not thinking straight. Anyway, I got one cuff on him, but he wouldn't let me cuff his other hand. I got mad and tried to force his other arm behind his back and into the handcuffs. We began to struggle, nothing big, just some wrestling around on the floor. Even though he was a little guy, I couldn't get the best of him, so I grabbed the knife to stab him, but he got loose and ran out the door.

'I was too drunk to chase him. What else could I do? I don't really remember what happened next. I think I passed out for a while until I heard a knock at the door. It was two big policemen and they were asking for the handcuff key. I could see the little black guy behind them. He had the one cuff on and said that he didn't want to prosecute – he just wanted the cuffs off.

'I fumbled around but couldn't find the damn key. The cops were getting impatient waiting at the door, so they entered and began to look around. I think one of them found my Polaroids and said something to his partner. The fat cop walked over to the refrigerator and started to open it, and I knew this was it, so I tried to stop him. I'm not sure what happened next. I just know that I got the shit beat out of me. I tried to fight back, but it didn't seem to faze them, and now here I am with you, Pat.'

House of horrors

Dahmer's confession ran to five pages. He signed it.

'It's over,' he said. 'I'm just going to have to learn to live with what I've done. It's funny, but in a way, I almost feel relieved.'

But it wasn't over. Dahmer then gave details of two more homicides he had forgotten about. The police then had the job of trying to identify all the victims.

'I never inquired into the personal lives of my victims. I really didn't want to know. It would have been difficult for me to carry out my plans if I had known too much about them. It would have gotten personal. I don't think I could have done it if I knew them too well.'

And there were more horrors to come.

'I bought a small floor freezer to store the bodies of my victims if I was pressed for time or too tired to dispose of them right away.'

In it, the police found flesh neatly trimmed and tenderized. He had been eating some of his victims.

'I began to feel that I needed more of a rush,' he said. 'I thought to myself, I want more. I wanted to keep this one, but I wanted him in me. I wanted him to become part of me. That's when the idea of eating part of his body occurred to me, so I severed his biceps, which were beautiful.'

He ate the heart first.

'It tasted spongy,' he said.

The biceps were chewy, so he used a meat tenderizer, then fried the flesh until it was medium-rare and sometimes added onions and mushrooms for flavour.

'It tasted like a fine cut of meat, like a filet mignon,' he said. However, he assured his employer, via the police, that he had not put human meat in the mixture at the chocolate factory.

'No,' he said. 'I didn't put anything into the candy.'

He bought chloroform to keep his victims alive and unconscious longer, together with formaldehyde to preserve their bodies and prevent them from smelling. One hot July, he had left a body he had been cuddling all night in his bed for three days. Then, when he pulled off the blanket, his victim's face was crawling with maggots.

It got worse.

'I was trying to come up with a way to keep them alive, but render them helpless and completely under my control. I thought if I could find a way to do this, I wouldn't have to kill anymore, so I began experimenting by drilling small holes in the top of their heads and injecting them with a syringe filled with various solutions while they were alive but still unconscious… I tried a boiling-water mix with the Soilex [cleaner]. Then I tried formaldehyde and even the muriatic acid.'

This was a preparation of dilute hydrochloric acid.

The living dead

After Dahmer had injected the various solutions into their brains, the victims woke up but were 'almost zombie-like'. Eventually, they all died.

One, who was only injected with boiling water, survived longer. When he woke up, Dahmer had to guide him around the apartment. He handcuffed this one to the bed when he went to work and he was still alive when he got home. Dahmer felt that, at last, he had found the right solution. He gave the man a shower and had sex with him.

The next day, he drugged him before going to work, but he was dead when Dahmer got home. He was disappointed. The experiment had failed.

'I really hoped there would be a way to keep them warm and alive, but compliant. It just didn't work out,' he said.

It seemed that Dahmer performed oral sex on his victims when they were still alive and only had anal sex with them after they were dead.

'I think it's because when they are dead, I have complete and total control over them,' he explained. 'I couldn't always reach orgasm with my live lovers, but I always climaxed after they were dead. Maybe it's because there is no pressure to perform when they're dead, so I can relax and concentrate on my own satisfaction.'

One body was completely flayed.

'I guess I was experimenting a little. I wanted to see if I could take off all his skin and save it,' Dahmer said. 'It did take a long time, about two hours. I used a small, very sharp paring knife… Anyway, I started by making an incision from the top of his head down the back of his neck. Then I carefully cut along the skull. It was a little tricky around the ears and nose…

'It was really no big deal. The skin is detachable, just like pulling the skin off a chicken you are about to cook.'

He said that he then peeled the facial skin away and wrapped it around his own face like a mask.

'I wanted to keep these guys with me. I didn't want them to leave. I loved them. That's why I killed them. That's why I saved their body parts. That's why I ate them – so they could become one with me. I thought if I could preserve this guy's skin, I could wrap myself in him. His outer shell would surround me. I would actually be in him. We would be one.'

Who was to blame?

Dahmer refused to say that he had been seized by some 'uncontrollable desire' to do what he did.

'I have one person to blame – the person sitting across from you, no one else,' he told Dr Fred Fosdal, who examined him. 'No one put a gun to my head. I had choices to make and I made the wrong choices. I could have made different choices in the past. It's obvious to me. If I had more foresight, if I had more motivation to find a career and worthwhile acts to fill my time rather than drinking my problems away.'

All 17 of his victims were eventually identified. Jeffrey Dahmer pleaded guilty on all counts. The jury found him sane on a split decision, 10-2. He wrote an apology to the judge, saying, 'Your Honor: It is now over. This has never been a case of trying to get free. I didn't ever want freedom. Frankly, I wanted death for myself. This was a case to tell the world that I did what I did, but not for reasons of hate. I hated no one. I knew I was sick or evil or both. Now, I believe I was sick. The doctors have told me about my sickness, and now I have some peace. I know how much harm I have caused. Thank God, there will be no more harm that I can do. I believe that only the Lord Jesus Christ can save me from my sins. I ask for no consideration.'

One of the many people he should have been apologizing to was Detective Pat Kennedy, whose marriage broke up under the strain of interrogating Dahmer. He related his ordeal in his book, *Grilling Dahmer*.

Dahmer was sentenced to life imprisonment for each of the murders, with an additional 150 years for concomitant crimes. On 28 November 1994, he was beaten to death in prison by a fellow inmate.

CHAPTER THREE

Dennis Nilsen

Even faced with overwhelming evidence of their horrific crimes, some psychopathic serial killers, like Ted Bundy, deny everything until the very last minute. Others, like Jeffrey Dahmer, confess everything to the cops. Some, again like Ted Bundy and Dennis Nilsen, tell all – or almost all – to journalists and writers. Nilsen, British cannibal killer who killed at least 12 between 1978 and 1983, went one better. Along with supplying material to author, Brian Masters, for his famous book *Killing for Company*, he spent his years in jail writing his autobiography. There were 6,000 pages of it, some 3.5 million words.

Nilsen was sexually abused by his grandfather as a child. Seeing the old man's body after he died, Nilsen became obsessed with death. A homosexual, he found gay life of the 1970s and 1980s transitory and ephemeral. He longed for love and sought a permanent relationship, so when lovers tried to leave him he killed them, then led a counterfeit domestic life with their dead body until decay set in.

Some partners he possessed more completely by eating their flesh. Bodies were usually disposed of by burying or burning. He was finally caught when flesh rendered by boiling and flushed down the lavatory blocked the drains.

Like Bundy and Dahmer, Nilsen was dependent on alcohol – in his case, usually Bacardi rum. Drink loosened their inhibitions about committing their ghastly crimes in the first place. It also helped them with the gruesome business of disposing of the body afterwards. Then, it became a coping mechanism, helping to numb their feelings, so they could live with the terrible things they had done.

In the beginning

In his autobiography, Nilsen expressed doubts about his paternity. While his father was away fighting with the Free Norwegian Forces during World War II, his mother entertained a number of soldiers posted to their hometown of Fraserburgh, Scotland. They divorced in 1948.

Nilsen said, 'For the most part, mine was a female-dominated world: mother, grandmother and aunt...

'My grandfather, however, had taken a shine to me. He was all that I could remember of any personalized, tactile contact, but this had a traumatic influence on my early development and on my future life...

'In all other ways, he was a good, moral man but a fantasist, whose inner world seized secret libidinous expression when the pressures of his life became stressful and his will proved helpless to prevail and resolve them.

'I arrived as that object of his problems and my presence "tempted" him as the devil tempts all men, who, in his religious mind, were all sinners. He levied and controlled his secret with the mind and body of a small, uncomprehending, male child soiled by bastardy.'

Persistent abuse

They would go off for long walks along the coast together, taking with them a flask of 'tea' – seemingly whisky – and stopping at a World War II pillbox.

'In that dark and cramped interior, he would give me a drink of the "tea" from his flask and I would feel sleepy as he pulled down my short trousers, held my penis and told me to urinate.

Dennis Nilsen arrives at court.

'What began as simple fondling developed and I was held in the rough embrace of this powerful influence, which ran its strong hands over my naked skin, fondling my buttocks and the small, shrivelled pinkie between my legs. I was in a ritualistic daze of incomprehension as he held my tiny hand in his during these events.

'He bathed me and sometimes took me to his bed and his finger penetrated me when it pleased him; and all this to the accompaniment of his soothing, reassuring noises of fevered contentment. He was an explosion of contradictions because, in tandem with the sexual abuse and its attending physical pain, there were all the material benefits which a grandfather bestowed on a young boy: ice cream, sweets, toys, etc.'

Nilsen said his grandfather might have been a paedophile, but he didn't remember him as threatening or oppressive.

'By the time I had started at the infant school, on a couple of occasions I had no control of my anus and, literally, shat my pants. I padded home feeling sore as the skitter dribbled, embarrassingly, down the leg of my short pants…

'As my awareness increased, I was forever silent in the presence of my grandfather when we were around others not party to our secret. I was both dependent on him and fearful of him; his tactility and embrace came at a price: no sweeties for bad boys. He was both ugly and comforting in turn and there was something monstrous in his odour.'

This ended when his grandfather had a heart attack. Nilsen was nearly six when his mother carried him through into the front room where his grandfather's body lay.

'Seeing him laid out in his coffin brought to me a great earthquake of excitement. I had lost the good aspect of him as well as the painful trauma of his abuse. I had wished him gone and he had gone and the guilt came from this and my excitement and sense of loss at viewing the mighty fallen, slumbering in that coffin in the room where I had been born. I was not that clear on the full meaning of death and felt that he could have still "got me" if I revealed our secret. As he lay there in his box that day, I was puzzled that he was ignoring me, as if he'd deserted me, and I hoped he would see me later when he was "better".'

Nilsen was told that his grandfather had gone to a better place, but it seemed to him that he was locked in a box six feet under the ground – which was apparently a good thing.

Cat killer

Soon, Nilsen had a second experience of death.

'I slipped a wire around a friendly cat's neck. I pulled up the cat by the wire attached to the cistern pipe and watched it struggle under its own weight. After it was dead, I prodded it and turned away, disgusted by my cruel behaviour. I wanted to see the reality and process of killing and death, though I wasn't excited sexually by the act and I have that guilt still with me today in its original, raw intensity.'

At the age of nine, Nilsen went to Fraserburgh Central School, where his sexuality began to reveal itself.

'I became obsessed by a boy I saw in the playground. He excited me from the first moment I laid eyes on him and I can only describe him as beautiful. I never spoke to him nor could I remember his name (if I ever knew it at all), but I watched him from afar in an obsessive state of fixation.'

He thought about him all the time but was too shy to even catch his eye. It was an all-consuming, intense love. But he was only too well aware that such feelings were not only wrong but abominable and must be kept secret. There was no escape, though.

'I remember one night when the whole family was watching the TV, a sequence of ballet came on. The male dancer wore tights that emphasized the huge bulge of his well-endowed genitalia (which drew my secret, rapt attention). My mother suddenly raised her voice in eruption, "Take that dirt off, it's just dirt!"'

Fantasy figures

At school, there was a picture of a French boy in their French textbook.

'As it was a black and white drawing, his skin was flawlessly marble white, and I couldn't take my eyes off his bare thighs where they met the grey material of his shorts. There was something else in his pose. It seemed to me to be faintly teasing, as if he were seducing me. Because my homosexuality had to be essentially hidden, I was well on the road to reliance on a fantasy existence. I would fantasize about other boys I'd seen and would spend much of my time alone.'

At home, he shared a bed with his older brother, Olav. When Olav was asleep, Nilsen said he pulled down his pyjamas and played with his penis and buttocks.

'One night, he showed signs of an erection, at which point I assumed he must have been awake. He never tried to stop me, nor did he ever say anything, even when it was clear that he was awake, and we never openly acknowledged what had been going on.'

Nilsen began to get an erection, too, and his brother nicknamed him 'Hen'. Then, a school friend showed him how to masturbate and Nilsen began practising in the lavatory at home. But there was no one he could share his secret with, 'which encouraged my further drift into fantasy. It seemed to me that, because of the proscriptions on same-sex relationships, I could only be physically intimate with boys if they were deeply asleep or unconscious. In order that I could express my power of intimacy over them, they would have to be powerless.'

And there were also the stars of the silver screen.

'I suppose James Stewart was one of the first... I found myself being drawn to stare at his crotch and bottom as he mounted his horse and sat astride it.'

Then, there were John Wayne and Gary Cooper. And, later, Anthony Perkins in *Psycho*.

'I was particularly gripped by a frisson of sexual excitement after the shower killing was over, from the close-up of Janet Leigh's staring eyes to her being put – clear-plastic-wrapped – into the car boot.'

It was not Leigh who excited him, but her extreme passivity. In his fantasy, Nilsen became the victim, while Perkins ravishes his naked body.

'I can hear him masturbating with one hand, while he fondles my bare buttocks with the other.'

One day an older boy pinned him down and sat astride his body.

'He had undone my shorts and fondled me, which excited a frisson in me: a mixture of rage and pleasure, the rage being attached to the fact that he had overpowered me.'

Then, he did the same to another boy.

'The difference being that I didn't undo his shorts but reached his privates by putting my hand up the inside of his thigh. It proved my power over another boy when I could render him powerless to prevent me grabbing his privates. It was an embryonic sex act... perhaps a rehearsal.'

In the Army

At school, Nilsen joined the Army Cadet Force. At a summer camp when he was 13, a sergeant took an interest in him and gave him two litre bottles of beer to drink. Nilsen passed out and, when he awoke in the morning, he believed that the man had interfered with him. His underpants were on inside out. At 15, he signed up for nine years in the Army. Posted to the British Army of the Rhine, he found himself naked in the bed of a young German.

'He must have carried me – unconscious – upstairs, undressed me and taken me to bed with him. I remembered nothing of the night before and kept away from him after that, though the thought of what might have happened excited me.'

Sometimes, he would feign unconsciousness in the hope that others would take advantage of him in his passive state – usually to be disappointed. When others got drunk, he said, 'I did experience a mild transitory buzz while undressing one or other of my young comrades.'

Posted to the war-torn British protectorate of Aden, one night he ill-advisedly took a taxi and woke up naked in the boot. When the cab stopped and the lid was opened by the driver, 'I grabbed the steel tyre lever and dealt him a sickening blow on the head. He went down like a felled ox as I got to my feet as keen and alert as a cat.'

He retrieved his clothes and put the driver's body in the boot, before being picked up by a foot patrol. His fantasies were now suffused with the thought of what the taxi driver would have done to him. Nilsen imagined him abusing his dead body the way his grandfather had before burying his corpse.

In the stockade, a guard showed Nilsen the scaffold. He hung on to the noose, while the guard released the trap door.

'I fell about a foot into the black chasm of the pit… I was buzzing with fear and excitement as I regained my stance, my eyes drawn to the gaping, black hole of eternity… It excited me that I had taken "the drop" of one of Her Majesty's gallows and was still around to appreciate it. On the way out, it dawned on me that the flat, shallow, concrete sink, with the single water tap at one end, was the post-mortem table for the examination of extinguished meat.'

Mirror image

Next, he was posted to the Persian Gulf, where Arab boys prostituted themselves. He also started a new practice that would lead him down the path to murder.

'In my room was a very large mirror and I came to be ever admiring myself in it. By positioning it at an angle, I could look at myself lying on the bed and I'd become aroused by my relaxed body. I imagined someone (the mirror's view) looking at me and lusting after my body.'

He also wanted to be the active party.

'I repositioned it, so that my head couldn't be seen reflected and I imagined myself in the dominant role, as well as the passive body in the mirror. The problem was that it just looked like me pretending to be asleep. I, therefore, had to make the image in the mirror look as unlike the real me as possible (and be as truly passive and helpless) for the imagined man to act dominantly upon it. I decided that the most passive and opposite from the real "living" me was the "dead", helpless me.'

He pretended that the 'other man' was a young lance corporal he fancied who had recently died in an accident.

'I stripped my bed and put the mattress on the floor. I wore my khaki shorts, desert boots and bush shirt. I sprinkled a lot of talcum powder over my hair, face, hands, legs and clothes to simulate dust and sand and to erase the colour. I rubbed charcoal under my eyes, then rubbed them to achieve a bloodshot appearance. I put three holes in a T-shirt and soaked them with a mixture of cochineal and saffron to look like I'd been shot dead.'

His fantasies went on to involve digging up a freshly interred corpse and having sex with it.

Seedy encounters

Back in Britain, he didn't have a lock on his door in the barracks. Resorting to the bathroom, the fantasy had to be adjusted accordingly.

'Old man on desert island fishes out body of young, drowned sailor and carries out the usual rituals, where I actually went as far as immersing myself in a filled bath, clad in my jeans and T-shirt. It was a sexually stimulating feeling, lying in wet clothes on the solid, tiled floor with the material hugging my skin.'

Later, he was drinking on the train back to Scotland with another soldier who passed out. Nilsen dragged him into the toilet.

'I unbuttoned the front of his trousers, pulled them down to his ankles and thrilled at the sight of his smooth, bare legs. I stood him up, close in my arms, and ran my hand down inside the back of his underpants to feel the round orbs of his buttocks. He felt warm and good and I liked the smell of him. I laid him back on the seat and began fondling his bare thighs, belly and privates. My penis was in full erection all this time and I would have put it into effect if it hadn't been for the persistent knocking on the door by passengers wanting to relieve themselves in the toilet.'

Nilsen was posted to Berlin, where 'one night out with the lads, I was so drunk that I ended up in a seedy room with a prostitute whom I screwed – or, more precisely, she screwed me… Apart from the wonderful shock of ejaculation, there was nothing in that set-up for me.'

At a dance in Bavaria, 'I even got snogging with a beautiful young girl who reminded me of Natalie Wood. Her family's own chaperones, however, angrily separated us as it may have been felt that, as a soldier, I had only one thing in mind.'

Twisted vision

But there were always the movies. In *True Grit*, there was a short scene that struck Nilsen as 'pure pornography'.

'It occurred when the Marshal, Rooster Cogburn (John Wayne), was bringing his load of shot outlaws into the settlement. The boss wanted to see who they were and there followed a lifting of the heads of the bodies, draped over the back of their horses. Nearest to the camera was the body of a teenage boy and the sight of his limp, top half being lifted by the hair and then released to flop back down again sent me into inner spasms of sexual frisson.'

This set off his old fantasy of the older man stripping the boy and washing his naked body. He had a drunken one-night stand with a middle-aged man, where a sore and bruised Nilsen alleged he had been raped. This, too, was transmuted into fantasy.

Nilsen bought a cine camera and shot footage of a friend who feigned being shot.

'I lingered the shot on him for a full five seconds and was excited by the passive image of him. Later, when he wasn't around, I would watch the footage of him and go to the bathroom to masturbate.'

Nilsen then tried to seduce the friend, before losing him to a sergeant. This resulted in a jealous fight. Nilsen was excited when his intended tried to strangle him.

Dead meat

Quitting the Army, Nilsen joined the Metropolitan Police. Seeking out a gay bar in Earls Court, he had a brief affair with a married man.

As part of police training, recruits had to visit a mortuary in Brent.

'The "sudden dead meat syndrome" didn't bother me in the least, having seen it all in Aden. I had also trained and qualified as a butcher; I could dissect a carcass of mutton down into its component joints (chops, saddle, etc.) in less than 20 minutes.

'What shocked me, upon entering the "butcher's shop" of Brent Mortuary, was that the dead bodies were treated with the same skilled and decisive casualness as carcasses of mutton; it was exactly like an Army butcher's shop. It was the first time in my life that I'd been fully confronted with the behind-the-scenes official view of dead people, treated like commodities of dead meat to be processed.'

The mortuary attendant was handling the naked body of a five-year-old girl.

'What produced a surge of sexual excitement in me was that, when he released her wrist, he let it flop, limply, against the naked thigh of the old man on the next trolley.'

Nilsen assumed the attendant would have sex with the little girl's corpse before it was eviscerated by the pathologist. As for himself, Nilsen took a pick-up back to a hotel where they drank until the boy passed out. Nilsen then undressed him and had sex with his inert body.

He cruised gay bars for other pick-ups.

'On the art front, I was fond of all paintings and sculptures featuring the nude, male figure, but the only painting to give me an instant erection was *The Raft of the Medusa* – once seen, never forgotten. It featured an image in full continuity with my predilection, i.e., man with naked dead boy lying on his lap.'

Nilsen soon became disillusioned with the notorious corruption of the Met in the 1970s. And when he caught two young men in flagrante in the back of a car, he could not bring himself to arrest them for gross indecency.

'It became clearly apparent that I couldn't reconcile my expanding gay lifestyle and aspirations while remaining a Metropolitan Police officer,' he said. He quit in December 1973.

He rented a room just off Cricklewood Broadway and got a job as a security guard. One of his colleagues had been an ARP warden in the war and had retrieved body parts from bombed buildings.

'I only worked a few shifts with him and the only time in our conversation when I experienced a moderate frisson of sexual excitement was when he said that he also had to prepare the bodies of some young American servicemen for dispatch to the States. That, again, conjured up my fantasy of naked, young men being washed and "attended to" by this old man.'

Bizarre striptease

One of the places he worked in had a library and Nilsen spent his time poring over gruesome pictures of dissected corpses in *The Manual of Medical Jurisprudence*.

On another assignment, he guarded a store of stuffed animals belonging to the Natural History Museum. He dyed his hair blond and, doing his rounds one night, he could not resist the impulse to strip.

'I stood there, naked and blond, before the rigid shell of this huge gorilla with outstretched arms. He was half-crouched and I walked between his arms and carefully draped my naked body over his shoulders, as my erection pulsated. I hung there, limp, feeling his solid, great, hairy body against my skin. Having no mirror, I imagined the sight of me being carried off, unconscious, in the arms of this great beast and I felt a great, relaxing peace come over me as I lay there for a few minutes imagining. When I came down, I examined where his penis should have been and was disappointed by the pathetic, little, hard stump on such a powerful creature. That seemed to deflate my ardour, in the discovery that he didn't have the means to satisfy me.'

After his landlady objected to him entertaining men in his room, Nilsen moved to Willesden Green.

'My fling with a gorilla was no basis for sexual happiness and I wondered where my life was taking me.'

He got a job as a clerical officer at the Jobcentre in Denmark Street just off Charing Cross Road. He shaved off his body hair and would go out on the pull at night, often successfully. He sought out 'sweet young things'. Otherwise he would go home with older men and pretend to pass out, so that he could be entirely passive while being 'domestically and sexually administered to'. Detaching himself, he would observe the 'proceedings' through half-closed eyes.

Failed relationships

In November 1975, he met 20-year-old David Gallichan.

'I called him Twinkle because he wasn't a very bright spark.'

They moved into a ground-floor flat together at 195 Melrose Avenue.

'I found my tactility with him more sexually exciting when he was unconscious than when he was aware. He had become so drunk one night that he flaked out, leaving himself to my total discretion to exploit his extreme passivity. He ceased to be David Gallichan at that moment and became the "created entity". I was then able to express a higher degree of physical and emotional tenderness on his sleeping form.'

Both Nilsen and Gallichan began having casual sex with other partners, sometimes swapping. One of Nilsen's pick-ups was 17-year-old David Painter. But when he put his arm round him in bed, Painter threw a fit. Fleeing, Painter broke a glass-panelled vestibule in the entrance hall and cut his arm. He was taken to hospital, while Nilsen was taken to Willesden Green police station to make a statement. Painter declined to press charges.

Nilsen's fantasies began to take on a more cinematic and bloodthirsty tone.

'All in slow motion and in full colour, I imagine what looks like a pool of blood on the ground. I rise up from this pool, naked with my arms outstretched in the crucified position. Naturally, I am covered in thick-clotting blood, with the droplets cascading off my body to the ground. In one outstretched hand, I hold a sword, which is pointing upwards. In the other outstretched hand, I am holding a naked, living and wriggling baby by the ankles.'

After Gallichan left him, Nilsen took in a sexually curious 17-year-old who had been brutally raped by two men on Hampstead Heath. Other flatmates moved in and out, but Nilsen found it impossible to form a stable relationship.

'I was desperate for some company. I'd been drinking at home before wandering out, very drunk, to the first pub that crossed my path: the Cricklewood Arms on Edgware Road. It was as far from being a gay bar as one could possibly get and was frequented, almost exclusively, by Irishmen. In my drunken haze, I got into conversation with an Irish youth, whom I later discovered was called Stephen Holmes.'

After closing time, they went back to Melrose Avenue. They ended up naked in bed together.

'My mind was seized with the panic that he would soon wake up and suddenly depart, after which I'd be plunged back into the despairing loneliness of a bleak, cold life.'

All or nothing

He recalled what happened when the stranger showed signs of waking up in his bed.

'I reached over and took the blue tie from the floor. His [Holmes'] back was towards me and I carefully slipped the tie under and around his sleeping neck. I quickly straddled him and, twisting the ends of the tie around my wrists, pulled tightly.'

Holmes tried to fight back but was soon unconscious. Nilsen then realized that, when Holmes came round, he would be in even more trouble.

'"I'll drown him," I thought. "It's too late to have second thoughts now; it's all or nothing."'

He ran into the kitchen, got a plastic bucket full of water and put Holmes' head in it.

'After a minute, the stream of air bubbles stopped… And so it was that I became a killer.'

Nilsen was grateful that he hardly knew the man he had killed.

'If I'd known him as a person with a clear identity, outside of inhibition-removing drink, I could not have laid a finger on him and I didn't want to kill him. It was the ritual with a passive male body that I craved…

'As I looked down at him, I had become my grandfather, looking down at my own passive, naked body.'

He picked up the corpse.

'Then I caught sight of us in the full-length mirror, his young head and arms hanging limply down my back like a rag doll.'

This aroused him.

'His young, naked body was totally at my disposal and, at the moment of his death, he had become the central prop in my fantasy.'

In Nilsen's imagination, he was the victim as well as the perpetrator.

'My mind had achieved an impossibility and had created a new reality: me carrying my own naked body and enjoying its absolute passivity.'

He spent a long time poring over the naked body.

Under the floorboards

'After the moral anguish of that first killing had abated, I was resigned to the fact that I was a killer and nothing could ever alter that truth.'

He hid the body under the floorboards. Later, he got it out again, washed it and dressed it in fresh underwear, then returned it to its hiding place.

'He remained there until the weather began to get warmer when I brought him up for dismemberment – a most sickening and unpleasant task. I cut the blackened, putrefied body into sizable parts and wrapped them up in cloth and small plastic bags before finally burning them in a fire at the bottom of the garden in August 1979.'

There was no knock on the door from the police, and no feeling of triumph at having got away with murder as he knew he could not escape from what he had done. Worse. It increased his social isolation, particularly during the time the body was under the floorboards.

Once the body had been disposed of, he brought a young Chinese student named Andrew Ho back to the flat for sex.

'I wanted to strangle him into unconsciousness and, to cover the offence, finish his unconscious body off afterwards. I put my hands around his neck and began choking him with all my strength, but he struggled like a tiger and I lost my grip more than once.'

Ho walloped him around the side of the head with a brass candlestick and made his escape. For months, Nilsen masturbated over what he would have done with him.

In December 1979, Nilsen picked up a Canadian student and committed what he called 'my second act of homicide'.

'Afterwards, Ken Ockenden laid back, there on the couch, and I gazed and gazed at him, wondering on the great mystery of where he'd gone and where he now was… That essence of the real Ken Ockenden had been removed by his death and the "dream boy" had entered the solid flesh of the "husk". I barely knew the real man; just a jumble of conversations, fuelled and fuddled by drink. Was his form now transformed into my brother, Olav, now no longer able to mock and reject me, passive and at my command?'

Perverted ritual

Then he began what became a ritual, the undressing and cleaning of the body, which aroused him. Often, he would do this naked. He would also shave off his victim's bodily hair, powder it with talc and apply lipstick, then examine and fondle the body, and masturbate over it.

'Then, the ritual was over. For this, I killed many men and no fire in the back garden could ever erase the memory of them from those that they'd loved and were loved by. I remained pathetic.'

Next, he strangled 16-year-old Martyn Duffey in May 1980.

'I didn't see the act as killing Martyn Duffey but as a necessary and compulsive act of removing his will and personality from his body, so that I could enjoy imbuing it with my own will and my own desires.'

Again, as he undressed the body, he imagined himself as the passive body being undressed.

'I had, again, become my grandfather, lavishing attention upon myself, supported by a prop of the desired partner.'

He would dress and undress the body repeatedly with the concomitant fondling and masturbation.

In August 1980, he picked up Douglas Stewart. Fearing that Stewart was going to rob him, Nilsen threatened him with a knife. He returned with the police, but did not make an official complaint.

'If he hadn't been so fit and alert, I would have strangled him in the follow-through and his body would have undoubtedly been subjected to the usual ritual.'

There were several men he picked up and used as props in his fantasies that did not come to harm. But there were others who did.

'There was one guy who was very drunk and whom I tried to strangle into full unconsciousness. He went limp and, as I was taking off his trousers as he lay in the armchair, he woke up, much to my surprise, and said, "Fuck me, please fuck me!" I was completely taken aback. He must have thought I was just playing a kinky sex game by putting a tie around his neck. He never knew the true nature of his situation.'

When he did succeed in subduing his victim, the mirror came into play.

'My highest peak of frisson was to stand before a full-length mirror, with the orange sidelights on, naked, holding the naked body with one arm under the knees and the other under its arms and back.'

Then, Nilsen moved house.

The big clean-up

'In the summer of 1981, I set about doing a last, mass dissection at Melrose Avenue, prior to my move to Cranley Gardens in Muswell Hill. Pulling decomposing bodies up from under the floorboards on to the kitchen floor, to cut them up, was a nasty and unpleasant task; the corpses were in varying stages of decay. In order to face this ordeal, I started drinking from a bottle of Bacardi rum and, by the time I was finished in the evening, the bottle was almost empty and I was practically legless. I put as much of the viscera as could fit into a space between a board and the fence on the right, near the bottom of the garden. I wrapped the other, mainly fleshy, parts of the bodies into smaller packages and put them back under the floorboards. The stench of the decaying flesh was still, even while pissed out of my mind, bad enough to cause me to periodically throw up.'

A bloody bag of entrails was dumped in nearby Gladstone Park.

'The dissection of decaying human meat did not have any excitement for me. It was just like butchering any carcass, though a normal animal carcass has not the repulsion of decayed human flesh.'

Nilsen also said that there was 'no suggestion of cannibalism' – at Melrose Avenue at least.

'When dissecting the corpses of the first two victims at Cranley Gardens (on the wooden board across the bath), I was able to reflect, rationally, on the culinary possibilities of fairly fresh, human meat, but the thought only engaged me for a few moments. When I sliced through human buttocks, the meat looked just like beef rump steaks, with the colour being slightly lighter than in beef. Similarly, the pieces boiled in the pot (on the stove at my flat in Cranley Gardens, in 1981) looked just like boiled beef.'

Nilsen thought that his victims might have had various diseases or that their flesh was contaminated by drug-taking.

'Also on moral grounds, I didn't think their flesh was suitable or fit for human consumption.'

If he had had the necessary chemicals, he said he would have preserved some parts of his victims – hands, penises and scrotums.

One-track mind

During his time at Cranley Gardens, he had several brushes with the law. On one occasion, he called the police after he thought he had discovered a dead body in a hole in the ground in Highgate Woods.

'Having a one-track mind at that stage imbued me with the possibility that I was not the only murderer in Muswell Hill.'

It turned out to be a large dog.

Dennis Nilsen's house at 23 Cranley Gardens in Muswell Hill. His attempt to dispose of his victims' bodies by flushing them down the toilet resulted in the drains being blocked – causing a neighbour to investigate and leading to his eventual arrest.

In April 1982, he picked up Carl Stottor, but he came as Nilsen tried to drown him in the bath.

'His premature ejaculation had ruined the flow of my fantasy, and so I put him to bed... Within the ritual of my fantasy need, he had served his passive role as a young, naked, male body to be ministered to and used.'

He thought of bludgeoning or stabbing another pick-up, but felt 'it was important not to damage his body, in such a way as to mar the purity of the image in my fantasy'. Besides, 'the noise of his last, desperate screams would, no doubt, wake up the whole street'.

Instead, Nilsen draped a damp towel over an electric fire beside the sleeping man in the hope that he would die from smoke inhalation. But the smoke woke him. He left unscathed the next day.

Then on 26 January 1983, Nilsen met his final victim, 20-year-old Stephen Sinclair. There was little conversation.

'I doubted that I'd understood a single word he'd said in his half-drugged Scots brogue.'

Nilsen thought he was on drugs.

'Soon, his pale blue eyes began to close above his pretty upturned nose and soft, pouting lips; the total possession of him beckoned me. He left with no more than the feeblest of struggles. It was the beginning of my last ritual of a possessive fantasy.'

On reflection, Nilsen had misgivings.

'Was to fondle his beautiful buttocks, or to take his nipples between my lips, being hateful and pornographic? Are tender caresses obscene? I thought not. What was irredeemably obscene was to kill Stephen Sinclair and use his corpse for a completely selfish purpose. I killed him and I used him and such homicide was a crime against humanity.'

Silent companion

That did not stop him using him again after he returned from work the following day. The next evening, Nilsen went out, leaving Sinclair's body sitting in an armchair. When he got home, he poured himself a drink and listened to some music.

'I sat back and contemplated what I'd done and what I'd become.'

Nilsen maintained that the act of killing was never an end in itself. He went on to list all the things he did not do to the bodies.

'Another point of great significance was that the more I was aware of my victims as individuals – with interesting personalities – the less likely they could be fit for use in my fantasies and rituals; they would have been unsuitable as an anonymous object or prop. It's hard to believe that more men survived my attacks than were killed and I was surprised that I wasn't arrested earlier.'

Nilsen was arrested on 9 February 1983 after the body parts he had boiled up and flushed down the lavatory blocked the drains. When the police turned up, they asked: 'How many bodies are we talking about, one or two?'

Nilsen replied 15 or 16 – it was only 12. He was convicted on six counts of murder and two of attempted murder. Nilsen was sentenced to life imprisonment and died in jail in 2018.

CHAPTER FOUR

Peter Sutcliffe

Peter Sutcliffe – aka the Yorkshire Ripper – terrorized the women of West Yorkshire between 1975 and 1980, leading to one of the biggest and most expensive manhunts in British history. He killed at least 13 women and attempted to murder seven others. Sutcliffe claimed that he had been told by God to kill prostitutes, but many of his victims were not sex workers. However, he was attracted to red light districts as the women there were vulnerable and less likely to attract the sympathy of the public or the police.

While admitting his homicidal campaign, when Sutcliffe went on trial at the Old Bailey on 5 May 1981, he pleaded not guilty to 13 charges of murder, but guilty to manslaughter on the grounds of diminished responsibility.

Sutcliffe took the stand on 11 May, and was asked by his defence attorney, James Chadwin QC, 'Is it right that you have admitted both to the police and by your pleas you have tendered in this court that you have killed 13 women?'

Sutcliffe confirmed that he had.

'You have pleaded guilty to attempting to kill seven other women?' asked Chadwin.

'Yes,' said Sutcliffe. He also admitted that it was his intent to kill 24-year-old prostitute Olivia Reivers, the woman who was in the car with him when he was arrested in Sheffield on 2 January.

Asked whether he wanted to get away after the police stopped him, he said, 'No. I could have done. I could have literally driven away before the police knew I had false number plates.'

He said that he wanted Miss Reivers to make a run for it, but he was not sure that he wanted to get away.

'Why didn't you make any attempt?' asked Chadwin.

'Because, by the time the police had arrived, I didn't feel the vengeance. I felt very little animosity at all towards Miss Reivers,' said Sutcliffe.

He then admitted that he was carrying a hammer – the same hammer he had been carrying in 1969 when he had been convicted of going equipped for theft.

Asked if he remembered an incident when he had left a friend's car, taking a sock with a stone in it with him, Sutcliffe replied, 'Yes. I hit a woman on the head with it.'

At the time, Sutcliffe said he had been searching for a prostitute who had tricked him out of money. He had followed the woman into a garage with the stone in the sock and attacked her.

He heard God's voice

Sutcliffe maintained that the inspiration for his murders came from a time when he worked at Bingley cemetery in the 1960s.

'What was it that happened at Bingley cemetery that you particularly remember?' Chadwin asked.

'Something that I felt was very wonderful at the time,' Sutcliffe said. 'I heard what I believed then, and believe now, to have been God's voice. I was in the process of digging a grave.'

He was in the Catholic section at the top of the cemetery at the time.

'I was digging and I just paused for a minute,' he said. 'It was very hard ground. I just heard something. It sounded like a voice similar to

Peter Sutcliffe leaving court on 5 January 1981.

a human voice, like an echo. I looked round to see if there was anyone there, but there was no one in sight. I was in the grave with my feet about five feet below the surface. There was no one in sight when I looked round from where I was. Then, I got out of the grave. The voice was not very clear. I got out and walked – the ground rose up. It was quite a steep slope. I walked to the top, but there was no one there at all. I heard again the same sound. It was like a voice saying something, but the words were all imposed on top of each other. I could not make them out; it was like echoes. The voices were coming directly in front of me from the top of a gravestone, which was Polish. I remember the name on the grave to this day. It was a man called Zipolski. Stanislaw Zipolski.'

Sutcliffe picked out the gravestone from a picture of the cemetery.

'It is the one with the statue of Christ on the top,' Sutcliffe said.

'Up to that moment in time had you ever heard a voice which you could not identify, a voice which you could not attach to some human source?' Chadwin asked.

'I had never heard this voice before. That was the first occasion,' Sutcliffe said.

Sutcliffe walked up to the grave because that was where the voice was coming from.

'What did you see on that grave when you looked at it?' asked Chadwin.

'I remember getting a message from the grave,' said Sutcliffe. 'I looked at several graves. I was looking round to determine where the sound came from. After looking at the grave, I walked back. I was kind of transfixed because of the voice. I just stepped back and I didn't know what to think at first.'

Then he read on the gravestone the Polish word '*Jejo*', which he assumed meant 'Jesus'. Asked whether that conveyed anything in particular to him, Sutcliffe said, 'Something did, because immediately afterwards as I stepped back to the path immediately in front of the grave, I saw what I took to be a definite message about the echoing voice. I always thought it was on the same grave.'

Asked what the message was, Mr Sutcliffe replied, 'I recall, Jesus was speaking to me.' He also remembered the phrase: 'We be the echo.'

'What is your recollection, not of what you heard, but of what you saw, that conveyed a message to you?' asked Chadwin.

Sutcliffe replied he read the words '*Wehvy*' and 'Echo' in Polish. 'Echo' was spelt '*Ecko*'.

'I thought the message on the gravestone was a direct message telling me it was the voice of Jesus speaking to me,' he said.

'It had a terrific impact on me,' said Sutcliffe. 'I went down the slope after standing there for a while. It was starting to rain. I remember going to the top of the slope overlooking the valley and I felt as though I had just experienced something fantastic. I looked across the valley and all around and thought of heaven and earth and how insignificant we all are. But I felt so important at the moment.'

'As a result of that experience, you felt important. Why did you feel important?' asked Chadwin.

'Because I felt for some reason I had been chosen to hear the words of God,' Sutcliffe said.

Asked what was being said to him, Sutcliffe replied, 'I could not tell at all. I had no idea what was being said… It was not the context of what was said, it was how it was said. It was so real, yet it was so unreal in quality.'

Who had he told about this experience?

'I told no one because I thought that if it was meant for everyone to hear they would hear,' said Sutcliffe. 'I felt I had been selected.' But he did not know why he'd been selected.

Brought up in the faith

Sutcliffe was a Roman Catholic and was a regular church-goer during his school years and for about two years afterwards. For about three years, he had been an altar-server and had been particularly interested in religion between the ages of 15½ and 17½, though his faith had since waned.

'Did it puzzle you why you were selected when you weren't active in any religious way?' asked Chadwin.

'Yes, it served to create even more puzzlement,' said Sutcliffe.

'Did you find any answer?'

'No. I tried but I couldn't find any reason why I should have been selected.'

'Who did you think that voice had come from?'

'I thought it was the voice of God.'

At no point between then and his appearance at the Old Bailey had he changed his mind.

'Have you ever stopped thinking that it was the voice of God?' asked Chadwin.

'I have stopped thinking that on several occasions for maybe a day or two, but never more than that,' said Sutcliffe. 'Then I got very depressed, especially if I read in the newspapers where somebody was supposed to be innocent and I had killed them. I had been quite convinced by the message I received that they were prostitutes. I would be very depressed by this, but had advice during the depression which lifted me out of the depression and I thought I was all right and I wasn't wrong. God didn't make mistakes and the newspapers did.'

Problems with his wife

Sutcliffe was asked about his wife, Sonia. They had met on St Valentine's Day in 1967 when she was 16 and still at grammar school.

'I did not go to her home for the first few months. I used to see her on Saturday and spent half the day and the evening with her,' Sutcliffe said.

They had been happy but, five months after they first met, when she had moved on to Bradford Technical College to do her A-levels, there was trouble between them.

'It was an involvement with another man,' Sutcliffe said. 'I was informed about it by my brother.'

Apparently, the other man had taken advantage of the fact that Sutcliffe could not take time off work to meet Sonia on weekdays. He confronted her and they argued.

Sutcliffe was already suffering from depression due to an earlier motorcycle accident. Someone had let his tyres down. He had skidded and hit a lamp-post head first. The depression dated back to 1965 or 1966. He did not remember being depressed before that.

It took about six months before he resolved the issue with Sonia when she gave him her word that she would not see the other guy anymore. In the meantime, he had been depressed – 'so depressed, in fact, that this led to my first encounter with a prostitute'.

'The quarrel with Sonia led to that encounter?' Chadwin asked.

'It did,' said Sutcliffe. 'I could not resolve the situation, no matter how I tried, because I saw her once a week and he was meeting her twice or three times during the week. When I saw her at weekends, she would tell me where she had been with him and I gathered that it must have been two or three times she had been with him. The only times I saw her was on Saturdays and we used to end up arguing.'

Asked why this had led to his first prostitute, he replied, 'I didn't know where I stood at all.'

As Sonia was not being faithful to him, he decided to be unfaithful himself.

'So, I got involved with my first prostitute,' he said. 'By this time, I knew there were prostitutes operating in Manningham Lane, Bradford because I'd seen them blatantly along the road. I approached one and she agreed to get into the car. We were on the way to her place and I realized what a coarse and vulgar person she was. By this time, we were practically there and I realized I didn't want anything to do with her. Before getting out of the car, I was trying to wriggle out of the situation, but I felt stupid as well.'

Nevertheless, the encounter went ahead.

'We went into the house and, when she got into the bedroom, she started taking her clothes off. She had told me it was £5 and, when we were in the car, I gave her a £10 note. She had told me that, when we got to her place, she would change it, but she started getting undressed and I asked her if she was going to change it. She said, "No," without looking at me. I said to her, "We'll call it off then," because I was only too glad to call it off. She didn't want to call it off and said we could get the note changed at the garage where I picked her up.'

This was when he was short-changed.

'We went back to the garage by car and she went inside and there were two chaps in there. I don't know whether she did this regularly, but she wouldn't come back out. One of the men came banging on the car roof when I refused to go away and the other escorted her away. There wasn't much I could do about it, but I was a bit annoyed and drove off.'

Lasting grievance

He was out of pocket and had nothing to show for it.

'It wasn't just the money. It was the fact that I felt annoyed because I wanted to resolve the situation with Sonia and hadn't done. It made me feel worse than ever.'

He said he had had no strong feelings about prostitutes and no desire to harm them up to that point.

'You said you felt not only had you lost your money, but that you felt worse because of the way you felt about Sonia?' said Chadwin.

'That is right,' said Sutcliffe. 'I felt more depressed as I felt I would feel better and that it would put me in a better frame of mind – but it had an adverse effect.'

Sutcliffe was so depressed he did not think he could go on. It was then he received messages from the voice.

'Then, I would get reassurance and was brought back to a state where I felt all right.'

He said he received hundreds of messages from the voice.

'Soon after this incident, my attitude towards prostitutes changed,' Sutcliffe said. 'I heard a voice which kept saying I had got to go on with a mission and it had a purpose. It was to remove the prostitutes. To get rid of them.'

Two or three weeks later, Sutcliffe saw the same prostitute with another woman, who he assumed was also a prostitute, in a Bradford public house.

'The two were talking to men in the pub and acting in the way you expect prostitutes to act,' said Sutcliffe. 'I went and approached the one I had been with three weeks earlier and told her that I hadn't forgotten about the incident and that she could put things right, so that there would be no hard feelings. I was giving her the opportunity to put things right and give back the payment I had made to her. She thought that this was a huge joke and, as luck would have it, she knew everybody in the place and went round telling them all about the incident. Before I knew what was happening, most of the people were having a good laugh.'

But no voice from God reassured him at the time.

'I heard it later when I was thinking all kinds of things about Sonia, perhaps not reasonable things to think about an innocent person,' he said. 'My mind was in turmoil and it could have passed through my mind that she was a prostitute as well, but I had reassurances that she wasn't and she was a good girl. They told me that the prostitutes were responsible for all the trouble.'

Sutcliffe did not know what had led him to believe that Sonia was a prostitute.

'The reassurances that she wasn't one still made me think along the lines that the prostitutes were responsible for everything,' said Sutcliffe.

Horrific violence

Four weeks after the confrontation in the pub, Sutcliffe attacked the woman with the stone in the sock.

Asked why, Sutcliffe said, 'I was attempting to kill her.'

'Why?'

'Because it was what I had to do. It was my mission.'

'Why?'

'Because I had been told they were the scum of the earth and had to be got rid of.'

'Who had told you?'

'God.'

'How did the message come to you?'

'Exactly as I just said. The same voice that I had been hearing for a matter of years.'

Asked how he knew the woman was a prostitute, Sutcliffe said, 'Because she was walking slowly along the kerb, looking at cars across the road. I think I was accompanied by another man.'

It was his friend, Trevor Birdsall.

'I got out of the car, went across the road and hit her,' Sutcliffe said. 'The force of the impact tore the toe off the sock and whatever was in it came out. I went back to the car and got in it.'

The police spoke to him, but no charges were brought.

'What did you feel about the fact that the lady whom you had hit with the sock had not pressed any charges and nothing had come of it?' asked Chadwin.

'I felt I was not meant to be caught or punished for the attempt,' said Sutcliffe.

Mental problems

Four weeks later, Sutcliffe had taken a hammer into the Manningham area, where he intended to kill a prostitute. He was apprehended and later convicted of going equipped for theft.

That was in 1969. He did not make another attempt until July 1975.

'How were you during that period 1969 to 1975 yourself?' asked Chadwin.

'Just the same,' said Sutcliffe. 'I suffered from depression. I came to live in London for a year and then I went to work on nights because I didn't like carrying on with the mission and I was in turmoil a great deal of the time.'

Sonia had accompanied him when he moved to London. She studied at MacMillan Teacher Training College at Deptford, but before she finished her teacher-training course, he returned to Bradford and got a job at Baird Television, Lidget Green.

Early in 1972, it had become apparent that Sonia had mental problems. Diagnosed with paranoid schizophrenia, she received treatment for about two or three months, then she suffered a relapse. Nevertheless, that episode seemed to be over by the time they got married in 1974.

Chadwin asked whether he was happy with Sonia. Sutcliffe said, 'Very much so, yes.'

When they were first married, they lived with Sonia's parents, which Sutcliffe said was 'difficult'. He kept suggesting that they should find somewhere on their own and move out, but Sonia's mother insisted they stay and save up for a house of their own.

Chadwin asked whether, between the years of 1969 and 1975, he had any doubts in his mind or asked himself about the mission. Sutcliffe said, 'Yes. Why it should be me that did it because I found it so difficult. When I went to live in London, I saw Sonia practically all the time and it never had the chance to get on top of me. Then, I went to work nights for about three years and this kept me busy every night, and at weekends I saw Sonia, so I was able to overcome it.'

The judge, Mr Justice Boreham, asked, 'In London, when you were seeing Sonia, you still got messages and resisted them, or what?'

'I didn't see any prostitutes,' Sutcliffe said. Then, in 1975, things changed.

'There was a voluntary redundancy scheme at work and I accepted that, so I was no longer on nights and I did the attack,' said Sutcliffe.

'I took the job on nights to keep myself away from the problem and having taken voluntary redundancy… it just became possible for me to carry on.'

On the attack

Chadwin asked whether he heard any voices in 1975.

'Yes. Before the attack on Anna Rogulskyj and during the time I worked on nights,' said Sutcliffe. 'They kept reminding me that I had a mission and wanted to know why I was on nights. I knew why I was on nights and stayed there as long as possible. The voice reminded me where I had to go next. I went in my car. I was told again that this was the night to go. It was about two days after hearing the first voice. I went there and it culminated in the attack on Anna Rogulskyj.'

He had taken a hammer and knife with him to nearby Keighley 'with the purpose to killing a prostitute'. He had hit Anna Rogulskyj on the head but had been disturbed by someone on the road. He did not think he had stabbed her. She survived after brain surgery, but she was psychologically traumatized by the attack.

Questioned about his attack on Olive Smelt in Halifax in 1975, he was asked why he had gone to Halifax.

'I went with Trevor Birdsall,' he said. 'We went for a couple of drinks. In one of the public houses, I had seen her and, on the way back, I saw her again. I said to Trevor that is a prostitute we saw in the public house.'

Sutcliffe stopped the car, got out and followed her down the street. Then he hit her.

'She fell down. I was going to kill her,' he said. 'I had the knife with me at that time. I was going to kill her, but I did not get the chance.'

He had been disturbed by an approaching car.

Sutcliffe said that, earlier that night, he had very strong feelings that he must kill a prostitute. But these feelings did not subside as he had hoped.

'Consequently, I did it with Trevor still in the car,' he said. 'I knew it was my mission. I heard voices – echoes. Sometimes it was the voice, sometimes an echo. Sometimes it was very clear, sometimes not.'

Again, Sutcliffe left his victim alive but badly injured and traumatized. Neither Anna Rogulskyj nor Olive Smelt have any links with prostitution, nor did Keighley or Halifax have red light districts.

Man on a mission

'I have dealt with the first two out of 20 incidents,' said Chadwin. 'The next one, two-and-a-half months later, was the first time you had killed. Did you go out intending to kill a prostitute that night?'

'Yes,' said Sutcliffe.

Asked why, Sutcliffe replied, 'The same reason as before. I was reminded it was my mission. It had to be done, so I went.'

'This time, you did kill,' prompted Chadwin.

'Yes,' said Sutcliffe.

'Did you enjoy striking the blows you struck?'

'No.'

'How did you feel about the physical act of striking those blows?' asked Chadwin.

'I found it very difficult, and I couldn't restrain myself. I could not do anything to stop myself,' said Sutcliffe.

'Why could you not stop yourself?'

'Because it was God who was controlling me.'

'How was he doing that?'

'Before doing it, I had to go through a terrible stage each time,' Sutcliffe explained. 'I was in absolute turmoil, I was doing everything I could do to fight it off, and asked why it should be me, until I eventually reached the stage where it was as if I was primed to do it.'

'Did you ever look forward to killing anyone with pleasure?' Chadwin asked.

'No, certainly not,' said Sutcliffe.

'Did you ever try to resist what you had been told to do?'

'There was one time,' Sutcliffe said. 'It is not in the records because nothing happened. I was on my way to the Leeds red light area. I got halfway there, and I was still in turmoil. I do not think I was quite in that state where I could possibly do it. I was arguing all the time. I was not always getting answers, and there was a lot I did not understand. I finally stopped the car and turned it round. I was shouting in the car. I set off back and was changing up and down the gearbox. Eventually, I got back home, locked the car in the garage, and went to bed. I felt a great sense of achievement at that stage.'

Sutcliffe claimed that he had been advised by God how to carry out each attack and murder, except for one. He had received no instructions about the murder of 21-year-old Yvonne Pearson. So, Chadwin asked him why he had murdered Pearson.

'Because of the directness of what she said and the way everything happened.'

'What did that convey to you?'

'That it was all arranged.'

'By whom?'

'By God.'

Chance encounter

Detailing the events that led up to the murder of Yvonne Pearson, Sutcliffe said, 'It was a sequence of events. I was simply on my way home from work at the time. As I was proceeding along Lumb Lane, a car backed out into the road. He obviously hadn't looked where he was going, and I had to stop suddenly. She came straight round the same corner the car had reversed from. She tapped on the window and opened the door. It was a complete surprise to me because I wasn't looking for a prostitute at all. She said, "Are you, you know, having business or something?" I asked her where she had sprung from because it happened so suddenly. She said, "It's good timing, or you can put it down to fate." Unfortunately for her, I thought this was my direct signal. I had a hammer on the car floor, and she said very little after that. I took her to where she wanted to go and, after I killed her, I apologized. I said I was sorry and she could get up, and that she would be all right.'

'Did you think she would be able to get up?' asked Chadwin.

'Oh, yes. I thought if I was wrong, she would be perfectly all right and she would be able to get up. She didn't and I realized it was meant to be.'

Chadwin told the court that Yvonne Pearson's skull was completely shattered.

'If that incident, so far as you were concerned, and all the other incidents, had not been arranged by God, would you have committed any of these attacks?' asked Chadwin.

'No,' said Sutcliffe.

He said he thought that the women he was attacking were 'prostitutes every time' – though this was not the case – and that he had never attacked a woman who he didn't think was a prostitute.

Asked whether he remembered the first time that he read in the newspapers that a victim of his was not a prostitute, Sutcliffe said, 'I am not sure – but I do remember the effect it had on me. Oh, yes, it was the MacDonald one in Leeds.'

'She is very clever, this one'

Jayne MacDonald was a 16-year-old shop assistant who had missed the last bus home after a night out with friends. But Sutcliffe said he had no doubt that she was a prostitute at the time he killed her.

'When you read in the press she was not, how did you feel?'

'I felt utterly shattered. Mentally, I could not accept it. I felt terrible – full of remorse.'

Sutcliffe admitted that once or twice he thought the woman he was attacking might not be a prostitute.

'But my feelings were completely overruled,' he said.

When Chadwin asked if he could identify these occasions, Sutcliffe said that one time was when he had murdered Josephine Whitaker in Halifax. She was a 19-year-old clerk.

'How did it come about that you entertained some doubt at the time but were reassured?' asked Chadwin.

'Because I was walking along chatting to her,' said Sutcliffe, 'and she was telling me things which I thought sounded completely innocent – she had been to her grandma's, she had bought her a watch, and liked to go horse-riding.'

But Sutcliffe said at the same time he was getting advice saying, '"This is a likely tale. She is really trying to play tricks on you. She is very clever, this one." The voice also said, "You are not going to fall for all this." It resulted in the killing eventually.'

Because he was being guided and protected by God, Sutcliffe said he wasn't frightened by the much-publicized search for the Yorkshire Ripper. 'I was intended to go on and carry on doing it all the time.'

'Intended by whom?'

'By God.'

The fake Ripper

The police received an anonymous letter from someone purporting to be the man responsible.

'I thought it was a diversion, so I could be left to carry on,' Sutcliffe said.

'Who did you think was responsible for this diversion, so you could carry on?'

'I thought it was an indirect act of God.'

Then the police received a cassette tape from a man with a Geordie accent claiming to be 'Jack', which they publicized. Did he remember that?

Six of Sutcliffe's victims (clockwise from top left): Vera Millward, Jayne MacDonald, Josephine Whitaker, Barbara Leach, Helen Rytka and Jean Royle.

'Yes, I heard the tape as well.'

Inquiries were then made on Wearside.

'It served to take a great deal of police investigation elsewhere,' said Sutcliffe.

He said he had nothing to do with the letter or the tape and did not know who had sent them. However, he did know people with Wearside accents. As a lorry driver, he had delivered steel in the area.

Sutcliffe was asked how many times he had been interviewed by the police in connection with the Yorkshire Ripper attacks.

'I can't remember how many times the police interviewed me,' he said. 'So many times I have lost count.'

'Did that frighten you?'

'No.'

'Did you think that the net was going to close in and that you would be caught?'

'It was a miracle that they didn't apprehend me earlier,' said Sutcliffe. 'They had the facts. They knew it was me. They had the facts for a long time, but then I knew why they didn't catch me.'

Asked why the police had not caught him, Sutcliffe replied, 'The police did not catch me before because everything was in God's hands. The way I escaped; the way they went away satisfied. There was no chance of them getting me.'

Of the police detectives, he said, 'One of them said they knew it was me and that he had no doubts at all, but he did go away. He must have had doubts. Another officer said that he knew it was me and he had a picture in front of him with my boot print on it.'

The missing fiver

After killing 42-year-old Emily Jackson, by hitting her on the head with his hammer and stabbing her 52 times, he had stamped on her thigh, leaving an impression. He had also left a boot print on the bedclothes of 32-year-old Patricia 'Tina' Atkinson-Mitra after killing her, hitting her four times on the head and stabbing her six times in the stomach.

'If he wasn't going to catch me, nobody ever would,' Sutcliffe said. 'The boots were new, and the soles and the heel were quite plain to see. The pattern was the same as he had on the picture.'

Chadwin then asked why Sutcliffe had returned to the scene of the killing of 20-year-old Jean Jordan to try and find the £5 note he had given her, which had come from his pay packet.

'Because I was told that this would point a finger directly at me and I would be traced,' said Sutcliffe, 'and the mission would have to stop unless I retrieved it.'

Who was he told by?

'By God. I thought it would probably be found and the voices told me that I ought to get it back. I was persuaded that it was perhaps better not to go back, because there were cars going in and out with prostitutes taking their clients into the allotments. I got the message that it would probably be too risky to go back, but couldn't understand why there was nothing in the news about the body being found.'

To Sutcliffe, it seemed impossible that the body still had not been discovered a week after the killing.

'By the following weekend, I was getting advice again to get the £5 note back,' he said. 'I realized the reason it had not been found was to give me the chance to go back and get the note.'

He didn't find the note when he went back. The police had eventually questioned him about it, but he had received further advice about the banknote.

'If it was traced back to me, to say I knew nothing about it and it would be all right,' he said. 'This did happen and, as it turned out, it was all right, although I could not see why I had not been discovered. But then again, God took care of the situation. I was puzzled that I did not get advice to where the £5 was when I was looking for it. I was quite often left to work things out for myself. I was not able to do so and this troubled me.'

Coming clean

When Sutcliffe's testimony resumed, Chadwin asked why he had placed the weapons he was carrying against a wall after he had been stopped with Olivia Reivers in Sheffield.

'Because they were obvious pointers to what my intentions were,' said Sutcliffe.

Chadwin then observed that, when Sutcliffe had been questioned by Detective Sergeant Des O'Boyle, he had not made any admission about the offences.

'I did not expect to be charged with murder even when I was caught with that prostitute in Sheffield,' Sutcliffe said. 'I had confidence in God. I gave a false name and address to the police, because the fact that I had been caught in that situation had no bearing on the mission being terminated whatsoever. Even when I was transferred from Sheffield to Dewsbury, I told the police lies because the point had not been reached where I could do otherwise. I was waiting and hoping that I would get advice from God.'

Only later when he was interview by DS O'Boyle again did he admit to being the Yorkshire Ripper.

'Yes, that's right.'

Asked what had made him admit he was the Yorkshire Ripper, Sutcliffe said, 'I had just been given a signal through the police that it was time to tell them.'

'How did that come about?' asked Chadwin.

'I was asked if I remembered going to the wall where I had parked the car in Sheffield and I realized that this was the time to tell them, because they were saying, in other words, that they had found the weapons I had hidden,' Sutcliffe said.

Then Chadwin said, 'I want you to explain to the jury; you have said you had been given the signal through the police that now was the time to tell them. You said through the police – from whom?'

'From God,' Sutcliffe said.

Following his arrest, had Sutcliffe heard any voices or received any more advice from God? Sutcliffe said he had not.

'At that stage, could you understand in your own mind why God was giving you a signal to tell the police?' asked Chadwin.

'No, I just realized that it was time to tell them everything I had done,' said Sutcliffe.

He had told the police that he was 'glad it was over'.

Why?

'Because I had been through terrible suffering all the time,' said Sutcliffe.

'In what way did you suffer?' asked Chadwin.

'Through having to go through with the mission against my will,' said Sutcliffe.

Chadwin reminded him that, at first, he had only admitted to the police 12 killings and two attempted murders. Asked whether he thought it would make things worse for him if he admitted to all 20 attacks, Sutcliffe said, 'No, not at all.'

Then Chadwin asked him why he did not mention the incident in Bingley cemetery.

'Because I thought that would lead them to find out about the mission,' said Sutcliffe. 'I didn't want them to find out about the mission. I was by no means convinced it was finished.'

Too much pressure

Asked how he envisaged his mission would continue, Sutcliffe stated, 'I had no definite thoughts in that direction. I did not know how, but God was in control of the situation, and anything was possible, so I said nothing about the cemetery. I did not want them to have the faintest idea about the vision at the cemetery,' he said.

When the police asked about a cord found in his possession, Sutcliffe had admitted attacking Dr Upadhya Bandara – who survived when a neighbour called the police – but not to the murder of 47-year-old civil servant, Marguerite Walls, who he had strangled with the cord.

'This was because there was so much pressure on me,' he said. 'But I was aware that admitting to this would probably open lots of new lines of inquiry that were nothing to do whatsoever with me and I thought I would deal with the ones which were attributed to me.'

He also said that he was not responsible for any other killing, where strangulation had been the cause of death.

Sutcliffe said he had used the cord in the attack on Dr Bandara, but he had not gone through with it.

'At the time, I was having messages,' he said. 'I simply heard the word "Stop" and I felt that way about it myself, so I left the scene. I was having a conflict and found it extremely horrible, the act of strangling her. That is when I heard the word, "Stop".'

After cross-examination passed to the prosecution, Sir Michael Havers QC, acting for the Crown, asked Sutcliffe, 'On the night of your arrest, you picked up Miss Reivers, intending to kill her?'

Sutcliffe agreed that had been his intention.

'Because God expected it?' Havers asked.

'Yes.'

'When did God last speak to you that night?'

'When I arrived and when I picked Miss Reivers up,' said Sutcliffe, 'and on the journey with the girl in the car.'

Sutcliffe agreed that he had suggested that Miss Reivers run away from his car when he was stopped by the police.

'Then, for a considerable time, you lied, and lied, and lied again,' said Havers.

'Yes.'

'All to protect yourself?'

'The mission.'

'All to protect Peter Sutcliffe?'

'Yes.'

Sir Michael then turned to the confession, which Sutcliffe had given to the police when he realized that they had found the hammer and knife he had been carrying.

'Did you say you were the Ripper because you knew the game was up?' he said.

'I knew it was the time to tell them.'

'Then, when found out, you decided to tell the truth, like any other criminal?'

'Like any criminal – not any other,' said Sutcliffe.

After receiving the message from God, Sutcliffe said he had told the police everything they wanted to know.

'No, Mr Sutcliffe,' Havers said. 'With God's message ringing in your ears, telling you to tell them everything, the first sentence you tell them is a lie.'

Sutcliffe's evasions

Sutcliffe said that it had been 'a great ordeal' for him to go through with his confession to the police. He admitted that, at first, he had not told them about the attempted murder of Dr Bandara or the murder of Marguerite Walls.

Sir Michael questioned Sutcliffe about the time he had first heard the voices when he was working as a gravedigger at Bingley cemetery. He said he found it remarkable that Sutcliffe had not told his wife Sonia about his revelation, nor the mother he was devoted to, nor his best friend.

'You didn't tell anyone until years and years had gone by and then you told them on the eighth interview in Armley Jail?' Havers said. 'What was so secret about this marvellous message?'

Havers continued, 'It must have been a great experience, this miracle – and you were transfixed – suddenly turns out to be instructing you to become a murderer?'

'Yes.'

'After you had been taunted by a prostitute, the first one you had met, you developed a hatred for her and her kind, that is a fact?' Havers asked.

Sutcliffe agreed.

'So, God very conveniently jumped on the bandwagon after that and said, "You have a divine mission, young Peter, to stalk the red light districts and avenge me by killing prostitutes,"' Havers said.

'It is a very colourful speech, sir, but it does not apply,' Sutcliffe replied.

Sir Michael asked whether he realized that his divine purpose in life had come about after he had been short-changed by a prostitute and 'humiliated, outraged and embarrassed'?

'That is after the incident when I got into a very depressed condition,' said Sutcliffe.

But he had not been to the doctor's. He had not told them about the blackouts he had had after his motorcycle accident.

Asked when he had realized that there could be a special defence involving his state of mind, Sutcliffe said, 'I can't be sure exactly.'

Sir Michael said that Sutcliffe must have heard about such a defence within a few days of being arrested on 2 January.

'You were telling your wife on 8 January that you were expected to get 30 years in prison, but if you could convince people you were mad then it would be ten years in a "loony bin".'

Cold-blooded murderer

Going back to the evidence, Sir Michael asked Sutcliffe to explain the different versions of the attack on 28-year-old mother-of-four Wilma McCann he had given. He had told police that he had killed her because he had lost his temper, while he had told the doctors he had left home with the purpose of killing a prostitute and that he always intended to kill her.

'Was it because you realized that what you had said about McCann would not be of much help to you if you wanted to pull the wool over the doctors' eyes?' Sir Michael asked.

Having decided to persuade the doctors he was mentally ill and that those he attacked were part of a mission, he knew that the story would collapse if he admitted to the doctors that he knew that five or six of the women he attacked were not prostitutes.

Havers then referred to the statement Sutcliffe made to the police about the killing of Josephine Whitaker, saying, 'I realized she was not a prostitute,' when he attacked her.

'Had you got to the stage where your lust for killing meant that everybody that you saw, if in a quiet spot, could meet their death at your hands?' Havers said.

'No,' said Sutcliffe.

Sir Michael again referred to Sutcliffe's statement in which he had admitted that, shortly before killing Miss Whitaker, he had said to her, 'You can't trust anyone these days.'

'Can you think of a more horrible and cynical thing to say to someone you were just about to murder?'

Sutcliffe agreed that his confession to the police about the attack on Miss Whitaker was that of 'a cold-blooded, calculated, sadistic murderer', but insisted that God had been giving him detailed instructions while the murder was taking place.

'Did God instruct you as far as Yvonne Pearson and the horsehair was concerned? Did he tell you to hide behind the garden wall when you were escaping after attacking Theresa Sykes?'

'Yes,' said Sutcliffe.

After he had bludgeoned Yvonne Pearson to death with a hammer, he had jumped on her chest and stuffed her mouth with horsehair from a discarded sofa he then hid her body under. Sixteen-year-old Theresa Sykes had been recovering from brain surgery when Sutcliffe was arrested. He had hidden after being interrupted by Theresa's boyfriend.

'Did you need God to tell you that unless you did hide you might be caught?'

'Maybe, maybe not. I am not sure.'

'When Yvonne Pearson was lying there gurgling and moaning and there was someone in a car nearby, with your high average intelligence you must have known you were in danger of being caught. You don't need God to tell you to ram it [the horsehair] down her throat?'

'No.'

'Did God tell you?'

'No.'

Sex fiend

Sutcliffe admitted that he removed some of his victims' clothes once they were unconscious 'to show them for what they were'. He denied that he had stabbed his victims 'in areas of sexual attraction in order to get sexual gratification', such as the breasts, and in one case in the vagina.

Why had he placed a piece of wood against Emily Jackson's vagina? 'Your case throughout has been: no sexual gratification, not doing it for lust or anything like that,' Havers said. He then drew attention to the case of 18-year-old Helen Rytka.

'You say you feel contaminated by the blood of a victim. You talk about your mission, and then surprise, surprise, here's pretty little Helen Rytka and you have sex with her. Why?'

'I didn't have sex,' said Sutcliffe. 'I entered her, but there was no action. It was to persuade her that everything would be all right.'

He said that he had had no choice. It had been important to keep her quiet as some taxi drivers were nearby.

'Of course you had a choice,' Havers said. 'God didn't tell you to put your penis in that girl's vagina.'

Sir Michael asked about the stabbing of 20-year-old student, Jacqueline Hill, in the eye with his screwdriver. Sutcliffe replied that her eyes had been 'staring at him accusingly'.

'You are not going to tell the jury she was not entitled to look accusingly at you?' said Havers.

Murder site of Helen Rytka being examined by crime reporter Norman Lucas and Assistant Chief Constable George Oldfield, 12 February 1978.

'Did it matter whether she was giving you an accusing look? You had God on your side.'

'Despite being told what to do, still partly inside I feel guilty,' said Sutcliffe.

'Did it occur to you that God is meant to be merciful, and you are killing people in a painful way?'

'I'm quite sure that the ways I killed them meant they never knew anything,' said Sutcliffe.

'You mean to say that your victims never felt anything as they were lying there moaning, groaning, gurgling, a screwdriver in the eye, stabbed, and one disembowelling?' said Havers.

Mr Justice Boreham then asked Sutcliffe why he had tried to cut off Jean Jordan's head with a hacksaw. Sutcliffe replied, 'Because she was in league with the Devil.'

Sutcliffe was then briefly re-examined by his defence counsel James Chadwin QC, where he again denied that he was trying to feign insanity and said that he could go on killing prostitutes if he got out.

'I still do not believe the mission is finished,' he said.

Fortunately, Peter Sutcliffe was not allowed out. He was found guilty of murder on all counts and sentenced to 20 concurrent sentences of life. After his trial, Sutcliffe admitted two more attacks, but it was deemed that prosecuting him for these offences was not in the public interest.

After two-and-a-half years in Parkhurst, Sutcliffe was diagnosed a paranoid schizophrenic and sent to Broadmoor. He was returned to prison in 2016 where he died four years later.

CHAPTER FIVE

Charles Manson

In 1969, the hippie dream of a world overflowing with 'peace and love' came crashing to earth. Despite the ongoing Vietnam War, Flower Power was in full swing. The younger generation were finding a new way to live. They took drugs, abandoned the traditional family, lived in communes, practised free love and valued music over everything.

In August 1969, there had been the free festival at Woodstock, upstate New York. But on the other side of the country there was a series of murders that exposed the darker side of the new hip lifestyle. They were committed by a drug-fuelled commune called, ironically, The Family, which was led by a petty criminal, drifter, hippie guru and would-be rock star named Charles Manson. With the senseless slaying of actress and movie star Sharon Tate, who was pregnant at the time, Manson petrified the population of Los Angeles.

In 1971, Manson was convicted of eight counts of first-degree murder and one count of conspiracy to commit murder. Asked if he was guilty of any murder or plotting any murders, he said, 'I killed a chicken once.'

Tough childhood

It has to be said that Charles Manson had little chance in life. His father had absconded long before he was born, so he blamed his mother for all his troubles. She was just 16 when she gave birth to him. When he was five, she went to prison and abandoned him.

'She got out of my life early and let me scuffle for myself,' he said. 'And then I became my own mother.'

After being passed round the family, Manson was made a ward of court, which led on to a life of crime.

'I spent the best part of my life in boy schools, prisons and reform schools because I had nobody,' he said.

Being small, just 5 ft 2 in (1.57 m), Manson had a hard time in prison. He was raped repeatedly by other prisoners, many of whom were black. This left him with a lifelong racial chip on his shoulder. To survive in prison, Manson had already become shifty, cunning and manipulative, and he found that the techniques of Scientology gave him control over other people. This stood him in good stead when he was released on 21 March 1967 after serving 12 years, on and off.

When he went to jail, it had been the 1950s. The world was conservative, restrained. By the time he came out, everything had changed. A new generation was turning on, tuning in and dropping out. He was 32 years old and headed for the centre of it all, San Francisco.

'Pretty little girls were running around every place with no panties or bras and asking for love,' Manson said. 'Grass and hallucinatory drugs were being handed to you on the streets. It was a different world than I had ever been in and one that I believed was too good to be true. It was a convict's dream.'

It was the 'Summer of Love'.

Hypnotic powers

When he arrived in San Francisco, he had just $30. He used it to buy a guitar and started busking on the street. Suddenly, he became something of a star in the hippy Haight-Ashbury district. People also flocked to him on the campus of the University of California at Berkeley. The youth of the world was turning against the establishment and 'straight' society. Suddenly, an institutionalized reject like Manson was all the rage. He soon discovered that he could use the manipulative powers he had learned in jail on the long-haired flower children that inhabited southern California. With his hypnotic stare, his unconventional lifestyle and the strange, meaningless phrases he babbled, he was the perfect hippie guru. He could combine Bible quotations he had learnt as a child with the rhetoric of Scientology.

He joined the Process Church founded by ex-Scientologist, Robert Sylvester DeGrimston Moore, who called his followers The Family. So, Manson began a Family of his own. He soon attracted fashionable middle-class girls who had taken the then chic option and dropped out of mainstream society. The first was Mary Brunner, a university librarian. She was naïve and impressionable, very much Manson's type. He stopped sleeping in the park and moved in with her. Soon, he picked up another girl called Darlene. By sleeping with Mary and Darlene, he found he could control both of them. Soon, Brunner found that she was sharing her apartment with 18 other women.

They moved to Los Angeles where he picked up more female followers, including Lynette 'Squeaky' Fromme, ex-girl scout Patricia Krenwinkel, high-school dropout Leslie Van Houten, topless dancer and Satanist Susan 'Sadie' Atkins and Linda Kasabian, who left her husband and two children and stole $5,000 from a friend to join. The women were initiated into Manson's bizarre cult by taking the hallucinogenic drug LSD and having sex with Manson in skilfully choreographed orgies.

There were also some docile male hangers-on, including former high-school football star Charles 'Tex' Watson and Bobby Beausoleil, former guitarist with the Digger band Orkustra and protégé of underground film-maker Kenneth Anger. They lived together on Spahn Ranch, an old Western movie set just outside Los Angeles.

Things start to go wrong

When Manson heard the Beatles' *White Album*, released in the US on 25 November 1968, he believed the tracks were full of messages

LA5)LOS ANGELES, Dec.2--CULT
LEADER?--Charles Manson, above,
34, was described today by the
Los Angeles Times and attorney
Richard Caballero as the leader of a quasireligious cult of
hippies, three of whom have
been arrested on murder warrants
issued in the slayings of actress Sharon Tate and four others
t her home. Manson is in jail

A mugshot of Charles Manson, taken in 1969.

directed at him and his Family. 'Sexy Sadie', he thought, was about Susan Atkins. 'Piggies' sneered at the 'pigs' – the police and the establishment. 'Blackbird' was a call for black people to revolt. And 'Revolution 9' meant Revelations, chapter nine, which talks of the coming of the Exterminating Angel.

Manson was blissfully unaware that a helter-skelter was a harmless British funfair ride and interpreted the track 'Helter Skelter' as heralding the inevitable race war, which Manson sought to provoke. In the resulting Armageddon, he thought, he and his followers would take over.

In the meantime, The Family kept going by stealing, selling drugs and the expectation that Manson's music was going to be as big as the Beatles'. However, Tex Watson had ripped off a black drug dealer named Bernard 'Lotsapoppa' Crowe. Manson went to see Crowe to sort things out. He took a gun. Then, things began to go very wrong.

'He was taking steps forward as I backtracked,' Manson said. 'After a couple of steps, I pulled the trigger. CLICK, nothing happened. Crowe smiled and I thought, "Oh fuck, what now?" Crowe laughed and put his meaty hands around my throat. By now, my back was up against the wall. He started squeezing and lifting me from the floor. I pulled the trigger again and got just another click – "Oh shit" – then, once more, I yanked on the trigger. Buried as it was in his stomach, the gun didn't make a loud report, but it was enough to change the whole atmosphere of the room.'

Crowe slid to the floor. Manson was sure that he had killed him. In fact, Crowe was not dead, merely wounded, but when it was reported that the body of a dead Black Panther had been found dumped in Los Angeles, Manson and The Family thought that the Panthers as well as the police were coming after them.

'During that time, I was convinced I had initiated a war with the blacks,' said Manson. 'The kids at the ranch caught the worst of my paranoia.'

Messiah complex

Manson was also afraid of going back to jail and decided the best thing was to move further out into the desert, where he told his followers that he was going to build a city.

'First things first; I went looking for some money I was owed for lyrics I had helped Dennis and his group with,' said Manson. Dennis was Dennis Wilson of the Beach Boys.

Manson went to see Dennis Wilson's agent. When he refused to pay up, Manson threatened to burn his house down. The agent said if Manson did not get out of his office, he was going to call a hitman. Manson then went to see record producer, Terry Melcher, who had said he was going to record him. But Melcher had heard about the shooting of Crowe and reneged.

Back at the Spahn Ranch, Manson conferred with Bobby Beausoleil, who had also been keen to be in on the music deal.

'Regardless of the setback with Melcher, we still believed our talent would someday be recognized and appreciated,' said Manson.

Another drug deal went wrong over some duff mescaline Beausoleil had bought off musician Gary Hinman, who refused to give the money back.

'I winked at Susan and jokingly told her, "Go kill him for me, Sadie,"' said Manson. 'The "go kill him" was said in jest. I never meant it, nor did I ever expect those words to be used against me in a courtroom.'

Manson denied ordering anyone to kill Hinman, but admitted telling Beausoleil, 'It's in your hands, handle it anyway you see fit.'

Beausoleil, Atkins and Brunner went to see Hinman. Later, Beausoleil phoned Manson to tell him that Hinman would not pay up, even though he had hit him and threatened him with a gun. Manson said he would come over. Then, he had an idea.

'Gary's a freak behind some kind of Japanese Buddhism, so I'll take my sword along and intimidate his ass with a display of oriental swordsmanship.'

Where's the money?

When Manson arrived at Hinman's house, Atkins and Brunner had searched it and found no money. Hinman then ordered them all to get out.

'I jumped back and made a sweep with my sword, cutting his jaw and ear,' said Manson. 'His hands automatically went up to cover the wound and blood dripped through his fingers.'

As Manson left, he said, 'Talk to him, maybe he'll remember where the money is.'

When Beausoleil, Atkins and Brunner returned two days later, they told Manson that Hinman was dead. Manson then left the ranch, fearing the police would turn up. Later, Manson discovered that Beausoleil had been arrested for Hinman's murder.

Back at the ranch, 'the girls had held their own meeting and discussed the best method of assisting Bobby. They decided that if murders similar to the Hinman slaying continued to occur, the police would begin to believe Bobby was not their man... I told them the plan was crazy and the police wouldn't go for it.'

According to Manson, Atkins said it would work because, at Hinman's house, she had written things on the wall like 'political piggy' and had drawn a panther's paw. If they did it again, the police would think that the Black Panthers had done it.

'It will be Helter Skelter,' she said.

Manson said he felt responsible. 'Since the shooting of Crowe, I had purposely initiated fear and resentment of blacks in the kids, but I had never wanted to start a war,' he said.

Afraid of going back to prison, Manson said he was leaving. According to his account, they begged him to stay, saying that they would not let him go back to jail.

'All right, I'll stay, but what you do is on your heads, not mine – understood?' he said.

Then two of Manson's girls – Mary Brunner and Sandy Good – were arrested for shopping using stolen credit cards.

'What the fuck is happening here?' Manson thought. 'One by one, this fucked-up society is stripping my loves from me. I'll show them! They made animals out of us – I'll unleash those animals – I'll give them so much fucking fear the people will be afraid to come out of their houses!'

He was still worried about Beausoleil, who, if found guilty of Hinman's murder, faced the gas chamber. Manson sought out Atkins and Kasabian, and told them, 'It's time to do something to help our brother.'

He rounded up Patricia Krenwinkel, then found Tex Watson.

'It's time to get something done for Bobby,' he told him. 'The girls are ready to do whatever is necessary. They don't have a plan or a place picked out, so it looks like it's going to be pretty much up to you. But I think it would be best to hit some of the rich pigs' places.'

'I am the Devil'

Manson told him to go to the neighbourhood where Terry Melcher used to live.

'Maybe even take some rope and hang somebody, like a reverse of the Ku Klux Klan thing. That way, it will put the heat on the blackies,' he said. 'Now I was so much a part of it, I might as well have been in the car with the others, knife and gun in hand.'

He blamed Watson for the Crowe shooting and the other three for the murder of Hinman.

'I felt that these two incidents were more behind the direction the old Ford was headed than any beliefs of Charles Manson,' he said. He hadn't twisted any arms. He wasn't sitting behind anyone with a gun to their head. Nevertheless, Helter Skelter was beginning.

'Fuck this world and everyone in it,' he thought. 'I'd give them something to open their eyes.'

Later that night, when the Family members returned, he was eager to hear the details of what they had done. Atkins was first out of the car. She flung her arms round Manson's neck and said, 'Oh, Charlie, we did it... I took my life for you.'

'Girl,' he said, 'what you did, you did for yourself.'

Watson explained that he had driven directly to Melcher's house, which was then being rented out to actress Sharon Tate. She was eight months pregnant. Her husband, film director Roman Polanski, was away filming, but coffee heiress Abigail Folger and her boyfriend, Polish writer Voytek Frykowski, were visiting, along with celebrity hairdresser, Jay Sebring.

As they walked up the driveway, a car approached. It was driven by 18-year-old Steven Parent. Watson pumped four bullets into his chest. Watson then cut his way through a screen on a window and climbed into the house. He let Atkins and Krenwinkel in. Kasabian lost her nerve at the last minute and stayed outside to keep watch.

Once inside the house, Manson's followers found Voytek Frykowski asleep on the couch. He woke to find a .22 in his face. He asked what they wanted.

'I am the Devil,' replied Watson. 'I am here to do the Devil's business. Give me your money.'

Rounding up Sharon Tate and her guests, Atkins told them that the house was simply being robbed and no harm would come to them. While she was tying them up, Jay Sebring broke free and made a lunge for the gun. Watson shot him in the armpit, then stabbed him four times.

Fearing they were all going to be killed, Frykowski attacked Watson, who beat him to the ground with the pistol butt. Then, in a frenzy, the girls stabbed Frykowski to death.

Abigail Folger made a break for it. Halfway across the lawn, Krenwinkel knocked her to the ground and Watson stabbed her to death. Sharon Tate begged for the life of her unborn child. Atkins showed no mercy. While Patricia Krenwinkel held Tate down, Atkins stabbed her 16 times. Tate's mutilated body was tied to Sebring's corpse. Watson then went around kicking and stabbing the lifeless bodies. The killers spread an American flag across the couch and wrote the word 'pig' on the front door in Sharon Tate's blood.

'A normal person would find the details of the night's events shocking and horrifying, but I had long ago stopped measuring myself by society's standards,' said Manson. 'I did not feel pity or compassion for the victims. My only concern was whether it resembled the Hinman killing. Would the police now have reason to believe that Bobby was not the slayer of Hinman?'

More victims

Manson watched the news on the TV the following morning and was disappointed that no one had made the connection to the murder of Gary Hinman, so the following night he went out with Watson, Atkins, Krenwinkel, Kasabian, Leslie Van Houten and Clem Grogan, a ranch hand on the Spahn Ranch who had joined the Family.

High on LSD, they were searching for random victims – 'so many of them that the deaths would shock not only the area but the whole world,' said Manson. 'We felt free of guilt. During our search for the right place to continue spreading fear and panic, we were not a bunch of uptight kids, but a singing, laughing group who might have been on their way to a party.'

Near Griffith Park, they went to a neighbourhood where they had once been to a party. They stopped in Waverly Drive outside the home of 44-year-old grocery store owner, Leno LaBianca, and his 38-year-old wife, Rosemary, who ran a fashionable dress shop.

'I walked up a long driveway and looked in a window,' said Manson. 'The only person I could see was a heavy-set guy about 45 years old who had fallen asleep while reading a newspaper. Satisfied that this was where the night's work would start, I went back to the car

Susan Atkins, Patricia Krenwinkel and Leslie Van Houten – three members of Manson's 'Family' responsible for the killing of Sharon Tate.

and got Tex. The two of us, me with a gun and Tex with a knife, went to the back door.'

It was open. Leno LaBianca woke to find a gun in his face. Manson assured him that he was not going to hurt him. Watson tied his hands behind his back, while Manson went into the bedroom to find his wife. She too was asleep.

'With a start, she sat up and grabbed for the covers in an effort to hide her body,' Manson said. 'She had a nightgown on, but to assist her in her modesty, I handed her a dress that was folded over the back of a chair.'

She pulled it on and asked what he was doing there.

'When we left the ranch, I had been geared to handle some of the dirty work,' said Manson. 'The kids had done their thing last night, and I was going to perform for them tonight. But these two people were not panicking or doing anything that might set off a surge of temper that would make me strike out at them. Somehow, I couldn't make that first move.'

He got Watson to take Mrs LaBianca back into the bedroom in the hope that her husband would make a lunge at him, so 'in defence I could do what had to be done'. He didn't, so Manson told Watson to guard them. He walked to the car and sent Krenwinkel and Van Houten back.

'Do it good,' Manson told them. 'Make sure it's done, so the pigs will put it together with Hinman and that pad last night.'

He also told them that he, Atkins, Kasabian and Grogan would go and find another house, while Watson and the others should hitchhike back to the ranch when they were finished.

Bottling out

Kasabian suggested that they make their next attack at Venice Beach, where someone she disliked lived. When they stopped outside the apartment house that Kasabian indicated, Manson handed the gun to Grogan, saying, 'You're the stud, help these girls do their thing. See you when you're finished.'

Yet again, Manson had bottled out.

Back at the ranch, he grabbed a sleeping bag and headed off.

'I didn't want to be a sitting duck,' he said.

Returning in the afternoon, he found kids from both groups. There was no one home at the apartment in Venice Beach, but Watson, Krenwinkel and Van Houten said they had done the 'number of numbers'. The LaBiancas had been killed with multiple stab wounds. The knife had been left in Mr LaBianca's neck, with a carving fork in his stomach.

They had used the victim's blood to write 'RISE' and 'DEATH TO PIGS' on the walls and 'HELTER SKELTER' on the fridge door. This provoked a media frenzy. But once again, no one connected the LaBianca and Tate murders to the death of Gary Hinman, nor apparently to Manson's Family.

'About the time I totally had relaxed from the tension of having murders hanging over my head, they nailed us,' Manson said. 'And man, it was the raid of raids. Al Capone, Pretty Boy Floyd, Ma Barker or Creepy Karpis never got half the action or attention the Los Angeles Sheriff's Office showered on us.'

He was jubilant, believing the police had busted them over the murder cases and he would be recognized as the 'guru' behind the killings.

'Come on, bastards – you're making history, but let's get through your moment of glory and get on with the charges,' he thought.

In fact, they were charged with auto theft. Even those charges were eventually dropped because of an invalid search warrant.

'It was like I was a god who could do no wrong,' Manson said.

Death of a 'snitch'

There was at least one more murder – Hollywood stuntman Donald 'Shorty' Shea, who had offered to help George Spahn, owner of the Spahn Ranch, evict The Family. He was killed on the orders of Manson who feared he had snitched to the police. Manson later claimed to have killed many more. The police thought at least 12 more; a cellmate said that Manson boasted of killing 35.

'Beginning with the murders, I allowed things to happen that I could have prevented,' he said. 'And I did, in fact, initiate the scene on Waverly Drive. The kids had their own purposes and motives for going to the Tate-Polanski house, but once done, the responsibility of it fell on my shoulders, like everything else.'

Atkins was booked as a suspect in the Hinman case, then Manson was charged with the Tate and LaBianca murders. Atkins had told cellmates of her involvement. According to Manson, she and her attorney then delivered her version to the DA in hope of securing immunity, then they sold the story to the *LA Times*. This, he said, projected him 'as love itself, magic music maker, a devil, a guru, Jesus'. He was the man who ordered her and others to kill.

'Shit, if there were any truth to what I was said to be capable of, I'd have been sitting in Hearst Castle with stereos in every room, listening to my own platinum albums,' he said.

But when his followers began hanging about outside the jail: 'I thought, "Hey, there might be something to all the charisma, love and magic trip Sadie was rapping about."'

If Atkins were to retract her allegation that Manson had told them to do it, he was not going to get convicted of killing anyone. At one time, Manson thought that she, Krenwinkel and Van Houten would take the rap, getting him off the hook. But Kasabian and Brunner got immunity and turned state's evidence, repeating Atkins' line that Manson had told them to do it.

Charles Manson being taken to court.

Weasel words

In his own defence, Manson made a rambling speech that lasted for more than an hour. As he had not been present for any of the murders, he addressed the charge of conspiracy.

'Is it a conspiracy that the music is telling youth to rise against the establishment because the establishment is rapidly destroying things?' he said. 'Why blame it on me? I didn't write the music.'

When it came to the murders – 'I don't recall saying to anyone, "Go get a knife and kill anyone" or anything.'

The defence for his co-defendants Atkins, Krenwinkel and Van Houten had been rested without giving them the chance to testify.

'If the girls come up here to testify and they said anything good about me,' he protested, 'you would have to reverse it and say that it was bad. You would have to say, "Well, he put the girls up to saying that. He put the girls up to not telling the truth."'

At the penalty hearings, Manson had shaved his head and trimmed his beard into a fork. 'I am the Devil,' he said, 'and the Devil always has a bald head.'

Manson and his co-defendants were sentenced to death. However, the following year, the death sentence was ruled to be unconstitutional, so their sentences were commuted to life. Manson was also convicted for the first-degree murder of Gary Hinman and the second-degree murder of Donald Shea. He died in jail in 2017.

CHAPTER SIX

Aileen Wuornos

Billed as 'America's First Female Serial Killer', Aileen Wuornos was a small-time criminal and prostitute, who robbed and killed seven of her male clients. During her ten years on death row, she wrote numerous letters (whose spelling I have corrected). In them, she denied being a serial killer. That was only a label the cops had used because of the number of men she killed.

'For serial killers – real ones stalk as often as they can,' she said. 'And if there's a cooling-off period, it's only in a matter of days. Not months. Plus, they're brutal in these deaths. These men were never tortured nor dismembered.'

She shot them.

Dead repairman

Her first victim was 51-year-old electronics repairman, Richard Mallory. On 31 November 1989, his car was found abandoned in Volusia County, Florida, his wallet and its contents scattered close by. Two weeks later, his body, fully clothed, was found in woods northwest of Daytona Beach. He had been shot three times with a .22 pistol. She claimed that she had killed him in self-defence.

'Richard Mallory raped me,' she said. 'He tied me to the steering wheel, then proceeded to vaginally and anally rape me. For nearly two hours. Then after he was done. He put rubbing alcohol he had in a

Visine [eye drop] bottle. [Up] the bottom, my nose, vagina and anus. This was excruciatingly painful. But more so in my ass. Because he tore me up bad. I never had sex like that. I never allowed exotic weird stuff while I hustled. Just clean stuff.'

Elsewhere, she described the rape even more graphically.

'Let me tell you what can happen in a rape. Your hair gets pulled out, he shoves his penis fully erected down your throat and bruises your oesophagus, as well as the roof and sides of the (inside cheeks) of your mouth... Also telling you, if you scratch my cock with your teeth, you're dead. Then he pulls your pussy hairs out, for additional pain, grabs your ass real hard like (kneading dough) as he's cramming his cock in you, same thing in anal screwing. Bites nipples, also, nearly cutting 'em off... as he's screwing you viciously, pounding as fast and as hard as he can... And also while all this is going on, threats are being made, and dirty talk at the most provocative profanity you could imagine.'

Even though Mallory had previously been convicted for attempted rape, Wuornos was convicted of first-degree murder and sentenced to death.

'I'm innocent!' she shouted at the jury. 'I was raped! I hope you get raped! Scumbags of America!'

Shot six times

On 1 June 1990, the naked corpse of 43-year-old David Spears was found in woodland 40 miles (60 km) north of Tampa. He had been missing since 19 May and had been shot six times with a .22-calibre weapon.

'Davis Spears, I was with from 1pm until 9 at night. He mentioned he had a sister who had a horse farm near Ocala. Me and him were drinkin' together all day. So we learned somewhat of each other. I believe when he learned I lived alone... This is where he got the idea of not paying but raping and beating me to death with the lead pipe full of cement. That no one would ever know what happened to me.'

Despite her claiming that she had acted in self-defence, she pleaded no contest, as she did in two other cases to 'get right with God'. In a rambling statement to the court, she said, 'I wanted to confess to you that Richard Mallory did violently rape me as I've told you. But these others did not, only began to start to.'

With the death of Spears on her hands, she had nothing to lose.

'I knew after his killing, it was over for me,' she said.

The killing was not going to stop, either. Forty-year-old Charles Carskaddon vanished on 31 May after leaving Bonneville, Missouri. His naked body was found north of Tampa on 6 June. He had been shot nine times with a .22 pistol and his car was discovered the following day. His personal belongings, including his .45 automatic, had been stolen. Despite the similarities in these cases, the police still refused to recognize that a serial killer was at work in Florida.

'Check this out. Carskaddon had hollow points in his .45... that's what he was gonna blow my brains out with. Right in the side of my temple. Now you can see why I unloaded my weapon, with nine shots in him, as he held his gun, trying to shoot me. Only thing is he forgot to slide a bullet into the chamber, when he slipped the clip in the handle. This he was trying to do. Slide it over as I was shooting him. I constantly shot him, so as to make him lose power, or drop his gun, so he couldn't slide it over.'

She later claimed that he also tried to rape her. Despite this, she pleaded guilty to the murder of Carskaddon and received another death sentence.

Missing body

Sixty-five-year-old Peter Siems was last seen when he left home near Palm Beach on 7 June, bound for Arkansas to visit relatives. On 4 July, his car was found, wrecked and abandoned, 200 miles (320 km) to the north. Witnesses to the crash were able to describe two women leaving the vehicle, one blond and one brunette. The blonde was bleeding

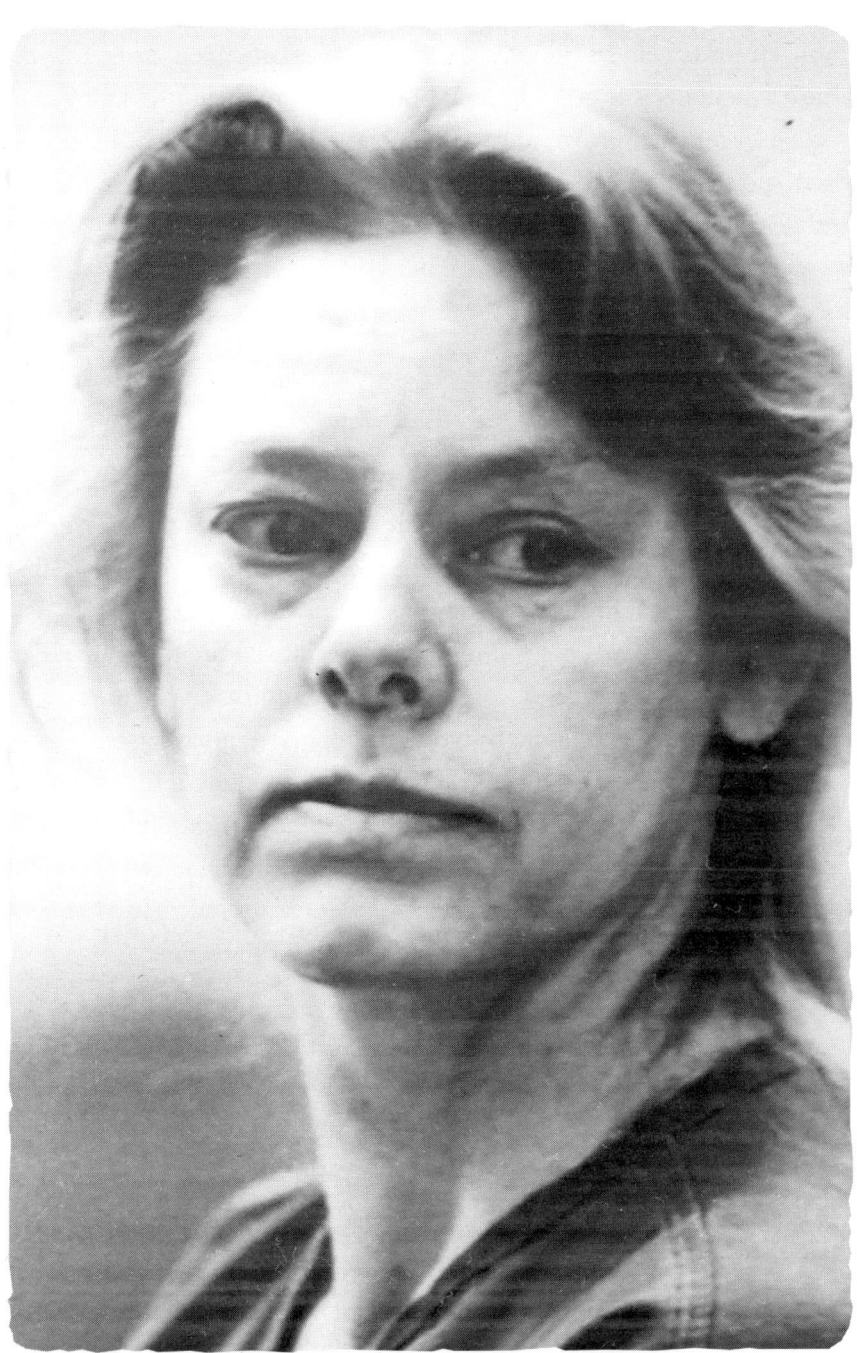

Aileen Wuornos.

from an injury, and a bloody palm print was obtained from the car trunk. As Siems was considerably older than the previous victims and was an evangelical missionary, it was thought unlikely that he would have knowingly picked up a prostitute. It seemed more likely that he had given a lift to two seemly harmless hitchhikers. According to leads, women answering the same description were seen near the other crime scenes. One was stocky, the other thin with a tattoo on her arm. Siems' body was never found.

'I was given a royal red-carpet treatment, because I was going to help them locate Siems' body. The search was a drag, because the cops... refused half the places I asked them to check and refused my overnight stay in jail to look more tomorrow. They were not interested. This is what led me to believe they just wanted a report to check, that they did, but no find. Because they already did but covered it up.'

As the body was not found, no charges were brought against her, though participating in the search was a tacit admission of guilt.

Fifty-year-old Eugene Burress was reported missing from Ocala, in central Florida, on 30 July. His empty truck was found the following day. Then, nearly a week later, his badly decomposed body, fully clothed, was discovered by picnickers in Ocala National Forest. He had been shot twice with a .22 pistol. His credit cards were scattered around and an empty cash bag from a local bank had been left at the scene.

Again, Wuornos pleaded no contest.

Also missing from Ocala, on 11 September, was Dick Humphreys, a 56-year-old retired police chief from Alabama. The following day, his clothed body was found, shot seven times with a .22-calibre weapon. His car was found two weeks later, some 100 miles (160 km) to the north, but it was not traced to Humphreys until 13 October, when his badge and other personal items were discovered 70 miles (113 km) to the southeast.

Wuornos admitted shooting him in the head, saying he was 'gurgling' and she felt sorry for him. Later, she said she had shot him in the neck and the bullet had travelled up to his brain. Even so, she pleaded no contest.

Naked trucker

Finally, the corpse of 60-year-old Walter Antonio, a trucker and reserve police officer from Marritt Island, on Florida's east coast, was discovered near the northwest coast on 19 November. He was naked apart from his socks. His clothes were later found in a neighbouring county and his car back east on 24 November. He had been shot three times in the back and once in the head, and his police badge, nightstick, handcuffs, handgun and flashlight had been stolen.

'Where I left him at, he should never have been found,' she said.

Told that Antonio was to be married, she said, 'Was he engaged? Him as old as he was. The ring! I doubt it. I couldn't even pawn it off but for 20 bucks.'

Mental blocks

The conviction for Antonio's murder gave Wuornos six death sentences in all.

She blamed her addiction to alcohol, or possibly some mental problems.

'What I mean is that, if I wasn't drunk [or] not drunk but psychological syndromes there, that blocked thought patterns, I would've held the gun with a smile, and said, "Next time just know that you may run into someone who won't put up with your shit." Period. If undressed, would of dressed and walked out. If dressed, just walked out, with the reassurance he continues to try any more assault, then I'll definitely shoot the fucker. But then I had mental blocks. See from alcohol influence… Being all cleaned up now and with a clear head, to properly rationalize. Never would of killed 'em … This is only [three] I can think of. I deeply regret shooting them. I know you're curious who. So I'll tell you. Siems, Antonio, Burress. The others were definite creeps, and showing signs, and/or physically on me, for serious bodily harm. Mallory I abhor. I know I'm gonna die, one way or another, be it natural [or] the chair. And do not give a damn about appeals… As for overturn sentences. Bullshit! when I know I'm innocent for various upon many of reasons.'

In a 2001 petition to the Florida Supreme Court, she stated her intention of dismissing her legal counsel and terminating all pending appeals. 'I killed those men,' she wrote, 'robbed them as cold as ice. And I'd do it again, too. There's no chance in keeping me alive or anything, because I'd kill again. I have hate crawling through my system… I am so sick of hearing this "she's crazy" stuff. I've been evaluated so many times. I'm competent, sane, and I'm trying to tell the truth. I'm one who seriously hates human life and would kill again.'

Wuornos had just given up. In the Mallory trial, the odds had been stacked against her. While, under Florida law, the prosecution was allowed to introduce evidence related to her other crimes to show a pattern of illegal activity, his previous conviction for attempted rape and serving a sentence in a maximum-security correctional institution for sex offenders was deemed inadmissible. After that, she pleaded no contest or guilty, so the cases did not get a hearing.

School of hard knocks

Although she complained that she did not get a fair trial in the case of Mallory, she did not fight the death sentence, so there was no appeal for mitigation. However, extenuating circumstances that could have led to mitigation of the death sentence did appear in the unfinished autobiography she wrote on death row. As a child, she suffered sexual abuse.

'My first run-in with rape would be at parties I was considered a stranger to. Out in Pontiac and Detroit,' she wrote, 'I'd find myself tied to a bed spread eagle, that is once I awoke and gang-raped. As I'd run into at least three of these brutal attacks at 13. Animals.'

Raped again while hitchhiking, she got pregnant at 14. The 'low life scum ball' concerned said he knew Aileen's father, who himself had been jailed for raping an eight-year-old boy.

'Then trying to hide it for six months... I was sent to an unwed home in Detroit. Only to then have to put him up for adoption once born.'

The child was large and she spent 24 hours in labour. She named the boy Keith, after her brother. 'The judge said that my child was adopted into a wealthy family and that the first name was kept.' She was sceptical.

Wuornos was brought up by her grandparents in Troy, Michigan. Then, her grandfather lost his job. 'I believe this is where the major problems in the house began. Him there 24/7 drunk. That's when [grandad] began to hit the bottle more than ever before.'

Her grandmother suffered from a thyroid condition. Her grandfather tried to ease her pain with beer, which gave her sclerosis of the liver. After she died, grandad committed suicide. Reduced to sleeping in the snow in the woods, Aileen ended up in a juvenile facility.

'It wouldn't be two days there, that I'd get locked down in a tiny cell away from the others for giving a Matron the finger. I believe they left me in there around a week or so.'

Nevertheless, she was allowed to make a field trip with the other girls.

'Arriving at a picnic area that was way out in the boonies, I kept looking around and saying to myself... How easy! And once everyone was pretty well occupied, I walked off. I must've been a good half mile when they finally noticed me missing! And then way in the distance, I could hear them calling my name as I just laughed and walked on.'

After being on the run for three weeks, she was sent to a Girls' Training School in Adrian, Michigan. She ran away again. Dogs were sent out after her and she hid up a tree, but after another three weeks she was caught and sent back to Adrian.

Cycle of misery

When she was released after 60 days, she headed off to try and find her old boyfriend. 'He had Beatles styled hair blond, blondish red moustache? Curious. He was my first. While I was at Adrian, he overdosed on heroin. Died.'

She had a girlfriend in Troy called Delia, who was soon supplanted by Dawn. 'We didn't hit parties as Delia and I did, but instead headed out to parks to cop drugs for personal use or to sell. Or we'd head out to the mall or the racetrack to panhandle and then hitchhike back to the park to buy some more drugs.'

They also hung out in a pool hall in nearby Rochester, where she learned to hustle, and a bowling alley, where she worked but also covertly sold drugs. Otherwise, she would make money as a hooker, which sometimes meant she could afford to stay in a cheap hotel.

Friends would put her up or she slept in a car. Sometimes she would have to sleep rough – even in the rain, sleet and snow, warmed with peppermint schnapps. She would wash in the restrooms at the gas station or in the local lake. Generally, she was treated as a pariah, being a girl who would sleep with everyone. That included her brother. But she was not cheap.

'No one, I repeat, no one ever got in my draws for cigarettes. I ripped off cigarettes from gas stations or bought them through hooking chink. Change from the wad of bucks I made. But I fucked no one for cigarettes. Geez! I wasn't that hard up! Stealing cigarettes was easy! And besides, if I was going to choose to fuck for something back then, since I was underage, it would have been for a case of beer or two, or liquor before a pack of cigarettes or a carton.'

A guy from high school offered to let her stay at his place.

'He got me drunk, he got me high. I passed out! He must have carried me to his bedroom. During my unconscious state, friends of his – some I knew, some I didn't – must have started to come over to party. Apparently, finding I was in the bedroom, they all conglomerated a plan of raping me. They tied my wrist to the bedpost. Spread eagle tied my ankles to the end bedpost. I awoke with come all over my chest, face, stomach, crotch (stinky all over), mouth hurting. They must have forced head on me in my unconscious state as well.'

When she screamed, they untied her. She got dressed and said she would go to the cops. They said, if she did, they would do the same to her friend.

On the run

Fed up with this, she headed for Florida where she could sleep out without being covered with snow. Hitchhiking with a friend, a trucker offered them accommodation rent-free, provided they cleaned it up. They stole and sold all his furniture and appliances.

Arriving in Fort Lauderdale around one or two in the morning, Wuornos was approached by a state trooper. 'He conned me into crashing out in an abandoned house…'

Later, he came back to check on her.

'… the conversation was quick and simple, stating he brought some of his buddies over to meet me, and not getting into a most humiliating and utter devastating event, I was gang-raped by his ass and other officers in uniform. After this ordeal, they warned me to keep my mouth shut, that I was lucky to be still alive and to leave Fort Lauderdale.'

She headed for West Palm Beach, then Albuquerque, New Mexico and Palm Springs. Staying with a family in the Colorado Rockies, she learned how to shoot.

Heading back to Michigan, she found a dismembered woman's body under the bridge, but when she tried to report it, no one was interested.

In Jeffersonville, Indiana, she got a job as a topless waitress. One of the patrons, who said he was a seventh-grade school teacher and a third-degree karate instructor, took her around the local nightclubs until the money ran out. He said he had to go home to get some more.

The house was remote, and he asked her in for a drink. She said she would rather stay in the car. He insisted, grabbed her arm and said, 'You're coming in whether you want to or not.'

When she struggled, he slapped her face. She hit him back and he slapped her a dozen times or more.

'I don't know how I broke free from this son of a bitch, but did, stumbling, then outta the car – looking desperately for an exit out – when I noticed a side door and took off running.'

He chased after her. When he caught up, she managed to knock him down and started kicking him in the face. She made off again and made it to the nearest house. But he caught up again. When he started assaulting her once more, residents called the cops.

'I found out I was some 50 miles outta town. I'd also find out the guy had been wanted for the murder of two teenage lovebirds who were both raped and killed, then put in a bathtub filled with cement and buried then in the back of another place he once lived in. Then to also find out he'd been likewise wanted for the beating and rape of a fellow officer's daughter, who wound up so beat up by the guy, that her face couldn't even be reconstructed with plastic surgery, he crushed her face in so bad.'

She was so badly beaten up she lost her job and went back on the road. Then she stayed with a family of Hell's Angels. Next, she got caught for driving without a licence. When she could not pay the fine, she made a run for it again.

Hitchhiking and hooking

She went to San Francisco to visit her brother Keith, who was dying of cancer. He left her $10,000, which she blew in a month. Then, she married a wealthy older guy, who she discovered was sexually perverted.

'He's lucky to be alive. Come near to killing him one night. Grabbed a .22 rifle, threw him on the floor, put my foot on his chest and the barrel of the rifle to his forehead, and said, "I want a divorce within 24 hours or I'll kill you." He left. I stayed two weeks in the condo. And finally, the divorce came through. Then left, hit the road…'

She then started combining hitchhiking with hooking – 'it's different altogether from "street hooking" and "topless joints" with all the sluts and trash.' The worst were the cops.

'I've only seen one cop go to jail recently for the murder of a business lady. A state trooper pulled her over. This same trooper tried to have me give him head in the woods. He pulled her over. Faked an arrest, handcuffed her, drove her to a medium strip on I-95. Raped her, then strangled her to death. Sick fucker, huh! There's many more I know.'

She worked as a topless dancer, then tried to join the Armed Forces, but failed the entrance test. Then, she was fired from her job as a welding inspector. By this time, she was drinking every day.

Hitchhiking in a snowstorm, she was propositioned by a john who wanted sex for free. When she explained that she was homeless, so that was not going to happen, he pulled out a gun. He told her to put out or get out.

'I sat there stunned and was amazed he still gave me an option with a gun, being pissed, too, that another pistol has been put in my face again. Wishing I had one of my own now to whip out back at him… I was getting fed up with it and began to get out.'

Concerned that she might freeze to death, he put the gun away and apologized. He had no money but was as horny as hell. She took pity on him, but only so she could stay in the warmth of the car until the storm blew over.

Alarming incidents

On another occasion, a trucker pulled a .357 Magnum on her.

'Glaring at me full of hate with it inches from my head. Saying, "Bitch I'm gonna get some of that pussy tonight!" I could see the bullets gleaming in the chamber. Having had just about enough of guns being thrown in my face. Blew and yelling away said, "Go ahead, you Mother fucker! Go ahead and shoot me, you son of a bitch! Shoot me – fucker! I ain't got nobody! No family! No home! Nothing motherfucker! So go ahead, Man. Shoot me, son of a bitch! Go ahead and shoooot meeeee. Godddaammmittttt!'"

His mouth fell open and he dropped the gun.

Another truck driver tried to sodomize her, holding a knife to her throat. She defused the situation.

'I knew that if I kept my cool I'd walk outta it all. Alive. So cut with the defense and dropped myself to his level, as low as I could go. Using the psychological method now to keep from serious stuff happening, sexually. Only for it to assist me, from sodomy.

'His imagination was running wild under his psycho craze of sexual rage. Pushing it way beyond the word exotic. Flat strange and fully retarded. Drumming up practically anything he could with his semen all over me. Insane! As he'd ejaculate and copulate to these continual orgasms just to spill it all over on me. Be it in my hair, my face, my chest or my stomach. Anywhere he could! And forcing me to hold his come in my mouth, slide it around, then swallow, when he said so. So, he was insanely bizarre and sick, to say the least. But grateful his sick ass self-erased any ideas of sodomy. I take it his ideas with the semen kept him from wanting faeces on it.'

She said this was three weeks before her 16th birthday.

'Then, to top off the humiliation that he wanted me to endure, forced me out of his rig right then and there at the rest area. Having to walk in front of all those people who could only guess what happened, which wasn't hard looking like death run over with bruises everywhere. And semen stuck on me from head to toe.'

Losing the fight

She would also get assaulted.

'I was outside of Georgia this car pulled over for me, having the driver next only to backhand me square in the face as hard as he could, just as soon as I opened the door, he then split just as quick.'

She was robbed too. One trucker drove off with her suitcase containing everything she owned, leaving her with just the clothes on her back. A waitress put her up until she could buy some more.

There were fights in bars and other guys in her life until, at 29, she had her first lesbian affair. But after spending $4,000 on her new love, the girl left her. When a guy in a local bar teased her about it, she beat him up and threw him out.

She then fell in love with Tyria Moore. To support the love of her life, Wuornos had continued working as a prostitute. Fed up with being robbed and assaulted, she began carrying a gun. The result was her killing spree.

The Last Resort bar in Port Orange, Florida, where Wuornos was arrested on 9 January 1991.

Moore eventually turned against Wuornos and testified against her in the Mallory trial. Nevertheless, before her execution by lethal injection on 9 October 2002, Wuornos said she was still in love with Moore.

'It was love beyond imaginable,' she said. 'Earthly words cannot describe how I felt about Tyria.'

CHAPTER SEVEN

David Berkowitz

Born Richard David Falco, David Richard Berkowitz plunged the city of New York into an era of terror with a killing spree in the mid-1970s. He killed six people and wounded seven others, shooting them in the street or in their cars. Unlike Peter Sutcliffe who claimed that he was killing because God told him to, Berkowitz said he did it at the behest of the Devil.

First known as 'The .44 Caliber Killer' because of the handgun he used, he later became renowned as the 'Son of Sam' – a sobriquet he adopted in letters to NYPD Captain Joseph Borelli, head of the task force assigned to capture the killer, and then to *New York Daily News* columnist, Jimmy Breslin.

The story began in 1975, when David's adoptive father, Nat Berkowitz, retired to Florida, leaving him all alone in New York. Renting a drab apartment in the Bronx, he wrote to his foster parent in November, saying,

Dear Dad,
It's cold and gloomy here in New York, but that's okay because the weather fits my mood – gloomy. Dad, the world is getting dark now. I can feel it more and more. The people, they are developing a hatred for me. You wouldn't believe how much some people hate me. Many of them want to kill me. I don't even know these people, but they still

hate me. Most of them are young. I walk down the street and they spit and kick at me. The girls call me ugly and they bother me the most. The guys just laugh. Anyhow, things will soon change for the better.

This display of paranoia should have been a warning. The following month, he began his murderous campaign.

Knifed in the back

On Christmas Eve 1975, he went out with a hunting knife tucked in the waistband of his dungarees. About 2 miles (3 km) from his apartment, in Co-Op City – the area where he had been brought up – he saw a woman in a long, navy-blue coat. The demons in his head, he said, told him, 'Get her. She has to be sacrificed.'

He raised the knife and struck her twice in the back. 'I had a job to do and I was doing it,' he said.

To no effect.

'I stabbed her, and she didn't do anything. She just turned and looked at me.'

The woman, who was Hispanic, has never been identified.

'It was terrible,' he said. 'She was screaming pitifully and I didn't know what the hell to do. It wasn't like the movies. In the movies, you sneak up on someone and they fall down quietly. Dead. It wasn't like that. She was staring at my knife. She wasn't dying.'

The screaming made him feel sick.

'There was so much confusion,' he said, 'and the screams were getting me scared.'

Berkowitz panicked and ran. Later, he told a psychiatrist that he did not understand why she was screaming. 'I wasn't going to rob her, or touch her, or rape her. I just wanted to kill her.'

Sadistic attack

The attack was never reported, and it was thought – hoped – that her thick coat protected her. However, the demons were not satisfied. A couple of blocks away, he attacked another young woman, 15-year-old schoolgirl, Michelle Forman. He stabbed her head from behind, then three times in the upper body. She turned and he struck her twice in the face. She was, he said, a 'pretty girl'. Then, as she fought back, he thought, 'Why aren't you dead?'

She screamed.

'I never heard anyone scream like that,' he said. 'The way she screamed constantly. I kept stabbing her and nothing would happen. She kept fighting harder and screaming more. I didn't know... I just ran off.'

Michelle survived and was discharged after a week in hospital, though one of her stab wounds had collapsed a lung. She did not recognize her attacker and her description was too vague to identify him in a city of 8.5 million people.

Cry of the demons

In January 1976, Berkowitz moved to a more comfortable apartment in a two-family house in Coligni Avenue, New Rochelle. The other residents, the owners Jack and Nann Cassara, had a German shepherd which barked and howled. Berkowitz had a job as a security guard.

'In the day, after my job at night, I'd come home to Coligni Avenue like at six-thirty in the morning,' he said. 'It would begin then, howling.'

Other dogs in the neighbourhood would join in. To Berkowitz, the howling was the cry of the demons, baying for the blood of women.

'On my days off, I heard it all night too. It made me scream. I used to scream out, begging for the noise to stop. It never did,' he said. 'The demons never stopped. I couldn't sleep. I had no strength to fight. I could barely drive. Coming home from work one night, I almost killed myself in the car. I needed sleep. I started to fall asleep on my job. I almost got fired. The demons wouldn't give me any peace.'

After three months, he moved to the neighbouring suburb of Yonkers.

'When I moved in, the Cassaras seemed very nice and quiet. But they tricked me. They lied,' he said. 'They said they were good people and they were lying. I thought they were members of the human race. They weren't! Suddenly, the Cassaras began to show up with demons. They began to howl and cry out. Blood and death! They called out the names of their masters! The Blood Monster, John Wheaties, General Jack Cosmo. I was able to sleep only an hour a night.'

In this new apartment in Pine Street, he hung blankets over his windows 'to prevent others from spying on me'.

Haunted by monsters

However, the area was by no means free of dogs. A neighbour, Sam Carr, had a large black Labrador. Berkowitz threw a Molotov cocktail at it in Carr's back garden.

Berkowitz was fascinated by cemeteries. He would visit the Jewish cemetery where his adoptive mother, Pearl, was buried. She had died of cancer when he was 14. He would also look for the graves where young girls were buried and speculated about whether they were pretty or not.

As a kid, he would play soldiers.

'I was always the German,' he said. 'I always wanted to be the guy who got shot down. When you play war, you know, the Germans always lose.'

This was, he said, to 'punish myself'.

Monsters also used to feature regularly.

'I used to watch horror movies on TV. All of them. Everything from Dracula to Godzilla. The other guys watched, too, but I was bothered more than they were. At 11, you know, or 12, the monsters haunted me. I couldn't sleep. I'd have to leave the light on. Sometimes, I'd run out of my room. I was so scared. Then I'd go sleep with my folks. When I had to do that, they seemed annoyed and angry.'

At 13, he said, the monsters stopped bothering him. Later, they came back to haunt him.

'The monsters planned to take me over, even when I was a kid. I'm almost certain that they're the same ones who got me later. Like they were with me. I think I was born so they could take me over.'

Then his adoptive mother died.

David Berkowitz shortly after his arrest in 1977.

'It was part of a master plan to break me down,' he said. 'It was no accident that she got cancer. My dad doesn't know about it, but it wasn't a natural thing. They [the demons] had plans for me. Like you know. Kill. Everybody circles around that.'

She had been poisoned, he thought.

'Somebody put something in her food,' he said. 'Evil forces. Poison… She went out one day to eat and she never came back.'

Paranoid thoughts

On a trip to see his father in Florida, he stopped at a diner where he noticed a platinum blonde sitting in a booth with her male companion running his hands up her thigh while she giggled. He sat at the other end of the counter.

'There is a force,' he said, 'to turn other people away from me. Somebody wants me destroyed, makes people dislike me and makes girls not be attracted to me in any way. If I had close friends or girlfriends, I would be able to resist the force. I would be able to resist, if I had people.'

Back in his motel room, he showered.

'I keep my body clean,' he said, 'so I don't get sick. I hate to feel dirty, or when my hair is all dried or stringy with flakes.'

In Florida, he spent a few evenings in singles bars, evidently with no success. With his father, he talked about his time at school.

'A lot of girls I hung around with came from Riverdale,' he said. 'We were all clumsy together. We didn't know how to do too much except kiss. If you wanted to make out, you just walked into a dark area.'

Soon Berkowitz found himself left behind.

'After a while, at Co-Op City there wasn't one girl who was a virgin,' he said. They were soon using drugs.

'I still wanted the girls, but I didn't want the other stuff, the drugs or anything,' he said. 'There was one girl that everyone scored with.'

Apparently, Berkowitz missed out there, too.

'Then, there was a girl before I went to the service. She was like 30 years old. Experienced. Wise. I mean she acted that way. But she was only 18.'

She said they never went further than kissing. He then spent 1971 to 1974 in the US Army, when, because of the war in Vietnam, the military was out of favour.

'I sort of lived like behind the times,' he said. 'I wanted to see some action, prove something to myself. It was rebellion then against parents, country and stuff. Kids were hippies and into drugs. I guess, then, I was very patriotic. Nobody else, except a couple of people, were.'

But by the time he had finished training, the war in Vietnam was winding down and he had been stationed in South Korea. It is unclear whether he used drugs or had sex with local prostitutes while he was there.

Gunning for trouble

From Florida, he moved on to Texas to see an old Army buddy in Houston where he could buy a .44 Bulldog pistol and three boxes of ammunition without a permit – something you could not do in New York. However, he had been granted a permit in New York to buy a rifle and, in January 1976, had bought a .45 semi-automatic Commando Mark III in Brooklyn.

'I thought the Commando would do just fine. But it's hard to conceal and I knew I had to get a handgun,' he said. Even so, he did not register the Bulldog in New York, which was illegal. He also bought a shotgun and two other rifles.

Quitting his job as a security guard, Berkowitz became a cab driver, which gave him the opportunity to learn the streets and avenues of the Bronx and Queens. But he was disturbed by what he thought were strange messages in the records he played over and over again. He also suffered from insomnia, which left him depressed. Unable to sleep, he put his .44 Bulldog in a paper bag and went out cruising the streets at night. He said he was watching people for 'some kind of signal to use the gun'.

On several occasions, the demons told him to 'get them', but he could recall how many times he 'failed on the job'. Still, the voices demanded blood. Then, at around 1am on 29 July 1976 in the Pelham Bay area of the Bronx, he spotted two young women sitting in a blue Oldsmobile.

'I was heading west on Buhre Avenue and I knew I had to get them,' he said. 'Those were my orders. I never saw them before until moments before the shooting.'

In for the kill

The two women were 19-year-old nurse, Jody Valenti, and 18-year-old Donna Lauria, an emergency medical technician.

'At the first corner, I turned around. There was a parking space there. It was an accident. But there was a parking space all set up waiting. Probably the most convenient location you could ask for.'

As Berkowitz approached the car, he told himself, 'I have a mission.' He said he did not want to murder but would do it 'as a kind of joke'.

He pulled the .44 from its paper bag and emptied the gun into the car, killing Donna Lauria instantly. Jody Valenti was shot in the thigh and survived. Berkowitz walked back to his Ford Galaxie, feeling that the shooting was 'a job well done'.

'Sam was pleased,' he said.

The following day, he learned the name of the girl he had killed in the *New York Post*. Seeing her picture in the paper, he became convinced he loved her.

'I never thought I killed her,' he said. 'I couldn't believe it. I just fired the gun, you know, at the car, at the windshield. I never knew she was shot.'

Nevertheless, he was 'elated' at his success.

'You just felt very good after you did it. It just happens to be satisfying, to get the source of blood. I felt that Sam was relieved. I came through… It felt good for a couple of weeks.'

It was a turning point.

'I no longer had any sympathy whatsoever for anybody. It's very strange. That's what worried me the most. I said, "Well, I just shot some girl to death and yet I don't feel." The demons are turning me into a soldier. A soldier can't stop every time he shoots someone and weep. He simply shoots the enemy. They were people I had to kill. I can't stop every time and weep over them. You have to be strong… you have to survive.'

He drew parallels with warfare.

'There are similarities,' he said. 'You're a soldier in both cases. In the United States Army, you can't stop to feel grief. You desensitize yourself.'

And he began to turn the murder of Donna Lauria on its head. She became his 'pretty princess' who the 6,000-year-old Sam had promised him as a wife. But Sam had lied.

'I don't know,' said Berkowitz. 'Maybe he would have given her to me eventually.'

He even tried to find her grave, believing she would somehow rise from the dead. Meanwhile, by mid-September, the demons had forced him to start cruising the streets in search of victims again.

'They broke me down. I felt sick, weak. They took a lot away from me. Things I can't get back anymore, like feelings for people. I remember once I used to be an auxiliary cop, you know, with the rescue squad at Co-Op City, beginning in October of 1970. I was risking my life then for another person.'

The Blood Monster

On the night of 19 October 1976, the demons were howling again.

'It was the Blood Monster,' Berkowitz said. 'Joquin the Joker.'

In Flushing, he pulled up behind a red Volkswagen at a stop sign. The driver had long hair and he could not tell if they were a man or a woman.

'I drove round. I saw the two of them had parked the car. I pulled around the corner and parked and I just walked up behind them. I walked up to the passenger's side.'

He drew the .44 Bulldog and, again, fired five times.

'Glass shattered. I stayed a couple of minutes watching.'

The Volkswagen took off. The driver, 20-year-old Carl Denaro, was shot in the back of the head. He was discharged from hospital two months later with a metal plate in his head. His companion, 18-year-old Rosemary Keenan, was terrified but unhurt.

On 26 November, Berkowitz again decided, 'It would be a night for hunting.' His car thought so too. 'It started right up, almost as if it knew I'd be looking again.'

Crossing the Bronx-Whitestone Bridge into Queens, he saw some girls in Hillside Avenue.

'I saw them standing with their friends and I parked. By the time I was able to get back and hide behind the lamp post, they started to walk. I followed. They saw me and walked faster. By the time I'd crossed the street and got to them, they'd gotten to one of the girl's houses. They knew I was behind them, and they tried to get in the door. One of the girls was wearing a maxi-coat and calf boots. The other a white furry coat and black jeans. She had blond kind of hair.

'I started across the grass to them. Everything was going right. They were right in front of me. I didn't want to get them frightened, so I began to ask them for directions. All the while getting closer.

'They turned back to the door for an instant, but it stayed locked. Then, they turned their heads to me. I had the gun out and pointed it in their direction. Then, I shot twice. They were both hit and fell on either side of the stoop.'

Berkowitz enjoyed the spectacle.

'It was just like it should be,' he said.

Sixteen-year-old Donna DeMasi was shot in the neck, but the wound was not life-threatening. Eighteen-year-old Joanne Lomino was hit in the back. She became a paraplegic.

Asked whether he intended to kill them, Berkowitz said yes. His excuse was that he was lonely.

'I am a sensitive person,' he said. 'I'm aware of things about me. I concern myself with something alive, like a bird or a plant. I love birds and plants. I always love nature. People too. Yet I was never able to relate to people. I was always a loner. I was a loner all that time.'

In 1975, Berkowitz had found his birth mother, Betty Falco, and his half-sister, Roslyn 'Roz' Rothenberg, who lived in Queens.

'One time I didn't hunt,' he said. 'Roz's family offered me the comfort of a life I never had. She had two daughters and her girls were everything to me. Also, there was my mom... my real mother.'

Evil cosmic dust

But the demons did not go away. There was Sam, who inhabited the body of Sam Carr, who was 'a speck of evil cosmic dust that has fallen to earth and flourished'. This was not a new phenomenon.

'He's been around since the beginning of time.'

It was a matter of concern.

'People should take me seriously. They should try and look into it. This Sam and his demons have been responsible for a lot of killing. The people should try to destroy Sam, if they can. It would be hard because Sam and the demons have been around for so long and they'll continue till the end, until God comes and destroys them in the last heroic final battle.'

Meanwhile, Berkowitz was not responsible.

'I am the Son of Sam. It wasn't me. It was Sam that was working through me. I mean, me and the Son of Sam, there's just one body, but we weren't the same people. Sam used me as his tool.'

That tool was about to go out on the hunt again.

'People really don't know anything. They don't know what's happening in the world. Take the United States. Some people think it's the President that has his hand moving everything. Others think it's the rich people like the Rockefellers or the Kennedys. But it's neither of them, you know. It's forces, God and Satan. They have their hands in the world. One day, God is going to bring peace into the world and there's going to be hope for mankind. I guess it was Satan's will for me to kill innocent people. It happens. Why? I don't know why. It just happened, but God will want to help people and in the end peace will win. People are dying every day in the most horrible ways. There's nothing we can do about it.'

He had no choice but to go along with it. 'Without Sam, I'm nothing,' he said.

Voices in his head

On 29 January 1977, he went out cruising Queens again. Around midnight, he parked near Forest Hills Long Island Railroad station and went for a walk. A couple were coming the other way.

'We just passed each other. We almost touched shoulders.'

He noticed that she was very pretty and heard the voices say, 'Get her and kill her.'

They were just getting into their Firebird when he approached.

'I don't remember what kind of car it was, a blue something. The engine was running and I just walked up from behind.'

Berkowitz just wanted to kill the girl.

'I wasn't told to kill him. I aimed for her head, you know, quick and efficient. I guess practice makes perfect. I was able to control the gun, physically. After walking up. I stood in front of the window, crouched slightly. I brought the gun up with two hands. I opened fire. Three shots were all I had to use.

'The glass flew into the car and I hit her. I just wanted to kill her, nothing more. I only used three of the five shells in the gun. There really wasn't any reason to use them all. I knew I had hit her. I had to save my ammunition.

'After I shot her, I began to run. I ran to my car. It was quite far away. It meant a long run for me. I ran past the Long Island Railroad and kept on going. I think I heard the car's horn blowing, and I think I heard the man get out. He began to scream. But, by that time, I was far away.'

He knew he had killed her.

'The voices stopped. I satisfied the demons' lust.'

Twenty-six-year-old secretary, Christine Freund, died later in hospital. Her fiancé, 30-year-old John Diel, only suffered minor injuries. The police began to associate the attack with earlier shootings as the same calibre gun had been used.

The body count was climbing, but that did not satisfy Berkowitz nor his demons.

'They kept needing blood and, if I didn't give them more blood when they wanted it, Sam would have done something really bad. Like killing multitudes. Once I remember his demons were howling all night long and I didn't do anything. The next day there was an earthquake. Where? Turkey, I think.'

Pretty women

At work, colleagues were talking about the .44-Calibre Killer. Berkowitz said, 'They gotta get that guy. He's really doing bad things.'

In the spring, he headed for Forest Hills again.

'I picked Queens because there are a lot of pretty women there,' he said. 'It seemed to me that Forest Hills was where the prettiest ones were.'

He was there in the evening on 8 March 1977, parked his car and went for a stroll when he saw a girl who was 'really beautiful'.

As she approached, he pulled his .44 and shot her 'somewhere in the face'.

'I only fired once, because once was all I needed,' he said.

The victim, 20-year-old student, Virginia Voskerichian, died instantly. Berkowitz ran for his car. He was spotted by a plain-clothes police patrol on the way. Although they did not suspect he was the .44 Caliber Killer, an officer was just about to get out to question him when the report of the shooting of a young woman three blocks away came on the radio, so the patrol headed off to answer the emergency call.

Berkowitz did not remember feeling frightened by this close encounter. Rather, he felt protected. 'Satan was creating illusions,' he said.

Task force

Detectives quickly realized that the murder of Virginia Voskerichian was the work of the .44-Calibre Killer and it was announced that a task force was being set up to catch him under Inspector Timothy Dowd, taking over command of the investigation from Captain Joseph Borrelli. Harking back to the Manson murders, Berkowitz called it the 'helter-skelter task force'.

'I read about this group they had started to get me,' he said. 'It was in the papers and on television. I remember Borrelli and Dowd. I followed them from that day on. Whenever anything was written about them, I read it. I also listened to the radio when it came up. I knew that they'd get me some day. The only question was how... and when.'

Or maybe not, Berkowitz decided after he began collecting press cuttings.

'The police couldn't see me. I was an illusion... someone other than David Berkowitz.'

Reading the coverage, Berkowitz felt no guilt nor any pity for the victims.

'After the shootings,' he said, 'I thought I might weep for some of the people killed. But I couldn't. It was all puzzling, you know. You hear so much news about victims, all the sob stories. In the United States, they show sob stories on TV so much. Women in tears. After a while, you don't feel anything.'

He was more than ever convinced of his mission to expose the 'conspiracy of evil'. The world needed to know about 'Sam, who was Satan, and Joquin the Joker, and that wretched building on Wicker Street in Yonkers, which was a Holiday Inn for demons, who travelled around the world.'

Wicker Street ran behind Pine Street, where Berkowitz lived.

To fulfil his mission, the world had to know about it, so on April Fools' day, he began writing a letter in block capital letters. It was addressed to Captain Borrelli, who had said, 'The killer must have something against women.'

Nightcrawler

On the evening of 17 April, he put the letter in his pocket, tucked his .44 in the belt of his jeans and went out on the hunt again. At 10pm, he was stopped during a routine traffic check and given a ticket for having no insurance card. This did not discourage him from cruising the streets.

At 3am, just three blocks from the home of Donna Lauria – the 'pretty princess' he was supposed to marry – he saw a couple embracing in a maroon Mercury Montego. He stopped, walked up to the car and fired four shots into it.

The man slumped forward lifeless. The woman slid backwards, moaning. Berkowitz was just about to finish her off when an approaching car disturbed him. He dropped the letter and ran back to his car, feeling 'flushed with power'. On the way home, he drove past Donna Lauria's home on Buhre Avenue and stopped off for a hamburger.

Eighteen-year-old Valentina Suriani, an aspiring actress and model, died at the scene. Twenty-year-old Alexander Esau died in hospital a few hours later.

After he was captured, Berkowitz was asked about the killing. He was embarrassed that he had, for the first time, killed a man. The demons had demanded it.

Why?

'General Jack Cosmo had a wife named Nancy Cosmo,' he said. 'Nancy Cosmo wanted some action too.'

Action?

'You know, sex,' he said. 'When the soul of a victim leaves the body, demons are right there. They snatch the souls and take them to the attic of 316 Warburton Avenue' – Sam Carr's address – 'or to the houses at 18 and 22 Wicker Street. They chain the souls and have sex with them forever. The demons take the victims' souls and drag them into houses and rape them and molest them. It's messy. It's brutal. There's no sleep for the victims' souls, no resting, no peace. Not now. Not for a while.'

Berkowitz's letter was recovered by the first uniformed police officer at the scene. It read,

Dear Captain Joseph Borrelli,

I am deeply hurt by your calling me a wemon [sic] hater. I am not. But I am a monster. I am the 'Son of Sam.' I am a little brat.

When father Sam gets drunk, he gets mean. He beats his family. Sometimes he ties me up to the back of the house. Other times he locks me in the garage. Sam loves to drink blood.

'Go out and kill' commands father Sam. Behind our house some rest. Mostly young – raped and slaughtered – their blood drained – just bones now. Papa Sam keeps me locked in the attic, too. I can't get out, but I look out the attic window and watch the world go by.

I feel like an outsider. I am on a different wavelength than everybody else – programmed too kill.

However, to stop me you must kill me. Attention all police: Shoot me first – shoot to kill or else. Keep out of my way or you will die!

Papa Sam is old now. He needs some blood to preserve his youth. He has had too many heart attacks. Too many heart attacks. 'Ugh, me hoot, it hurts, sonny boy.'

I miss my pretty princess most of all. She's resting in our ladies house but I'll see her soon.

I am the 'Monster' – 'Beelzebub' – the 'Chubby Behemouth'. I love to hunt. Prowling the streets looking for fair game – tasty meat. The wemon of Queens are prettyist of all. I must be the water they drink. I live for the hunt – my life. Blood for papa.

Mr Borrelli, sir, I dont want to kill anymore, no sir, no more but I must, 'honour thy father.' I want to make love to the world. I love people. I don't belong on Earth. Return me to yahoos.

To the people of Queens, I love you. And I want to wish all of you a happy Easter. May God bless you in this life and in the next and for now I say goodbye and goodnight.

Police: Let me haunt you with these words; I'll be back! I'll be back! To be interrpreted as – bang, bang, bang, bank, bang – ugh!!

Yours in murder

Mr Monster

Get thee hence, Satan

The .44-Calibre Killer now became the Son of Sam. The name caught on and a fresh wave of fear broke over New York.

Berkowitz said he hoped that the letter would lead the police to Sam Carr. Once Satan was arrested, he – Berkowitz – would be free of his control and would be able to stop killing. Soon he realized that this was futile.

'Nothing could hurt Sam. He knew the letter wouldn't hurt him. You see, he knew the police. I thought the police would be able to piece things together. Sam knew they wouldn't. If he thought they could, something would have happened. I'm telling you my car would have been smashed up.'

On 10 April, Sam Carr had received an anonymous letter complaining about the barking of his family's Labrador. 'Our lives have been torn apart because of that dog,' the letter read. It was signed: 'A Citizen'.

Two days after the murder of Valentina Suriani and Alexander Esau, on 19 April, Carr received another one. It read,

> *I have asked you kindly to stop that dog from howling all day long, yet he continues to do so. I pleaded with you. I told you how this is destroying my family. We have no peace, no rest.*
>
> *Now I know what king of a person you are and what kind of family you are. You are cruel and inconsiderate. You have no love for other human beings. Your selfish, Mr Carr. My life is destroyed now. I have nothing to lose anymore. I can see that there shall be no peace in my life, or my families life until I end yours.*

Carr called the police. A week later, on 27 April, he heard a gun being fired. He found his Labrador had been shot in the backyard. He reported this to the police who were now on the case.

Another weird letter

The Son of Sam was the main topic of conversation at the mail sorting office where Berkowitz now worked. This began to annoy him.

'Son of Sam, Son of Sam. They are making jokes, you know. I told them, "Don't make jokes, 'cause he'll get you, man." It's like making fun of the devil.'

At the *New York Daily News*, columnist Jimmy Breslin was taking a particular interest in the Son of Sam. He lived in Forest Hills, within a mile or two of Berkowitz's murders.

On the afternoon of 1 June 1977, he received a letter, which read,

Hello from the gutters of N.Y.C. which are filled with dog manure, vomit, stale wine, urine and blood. Hello from the sewers of N.Y.C. which swallow up these delicacies when they are washed away by the sweeper trucks.

Hello from the cracks in the sidewalks of N.Y.C. and from the ants that dwell in these cracks and feed in the dried blood of the dead that has settled into the cracks.

J.B., I'm just dropping you a line to let you know that I appreciate your interest in those recent and horrendous .44 killings. I also want to tell you that I read your column daily and I find it quite informative.

Tell me Jim, what will you have for July twenty-ninth? You can forget about me if you like because I don't care for publicity. However you must not forget Donna Lauria and you cannot let the people forget her either. She was a very, very sweet girl but Sam's a thirsty lad and he won't let me stop killing until he gets his fill of blood.

Mr Breslin, sir, don't think that because you haven't heard from me for a while that I went to sleep. No, rather, I am still here. Like a spirit roaming the night. Thirsty, hungry, seldom stopping to rest; anxious to please Sam. I love my work. Now, the void has been filled.

Perhaps we shall meet face to face someday or perhaps I will be blown away by cops with smoking .38's. Whatever, if I shall be fortunate enough to meet you I will tell you all about Sam if you like and I will introduce you to him. His name is 'Sam the terrible.'

Not knowing what the future holds I shall say farewell and I will see you at the next job. Or should I say you will see my handiwork at the next job?

Remember Ms Lauria. Thank you.

In their blood and from the gutter 'Sam's creation' .44

Here are some names to help you along. Forward them to the inspector for use by N.C.I.C

The Duke of Death

The Wicked King Wicker

The Twenty Two Disciples of Hell

And lastly John 'Wheaties' – Rapist and Suffocator of Young Girls.

PS: Please inform all the detectives working the slaying to remain.

P.S: JB, Please inform all the detectives working the case that I wish them the best of luck. Keep 'em digging, drive on, think positive, get off your butts, knock on coffins, etc.

Upon my capture I promise to buy all the guys working the case a new pair of shoes if I can get up the money.

Son of Sam

The NCIC is the National Crime Information Center, the US's computerized index of crime and criminals. And 'John Wheaties' may refer to one of the sons of Sam Carr and wife Frances, whose children were Michael, John and daughter, Wheat.

'I wrote Mr Breslin because he had an obsession with the shootings,' Berkowitz later explained. 'I also wanted him to write about Donna Lauria because the newspapers did not cover her properly... I felt a mystical attachment to her that I can't explain.'

Disturbed ramblings

After his capture, Berkowitz explained how he was trying to help the police with his letters.

'The Duke of Death lives at 22 Wicker Street along with Wicker King Wicker. The King is over the Duke, but still just an officer under Sam, much lower than General Cosmo. It's no accident either, Wicker... wicked. Do you notice the connection? It's just what they are, wicked, wicked demons. They changed the name to Wicker Street. The Wicked Wicker. And John Wheaties, he lives in the same house as Sam Carr, at 316 Warburton Avenue.'

However, he had not given the addresses in the letter, so the police had nothing to go on.

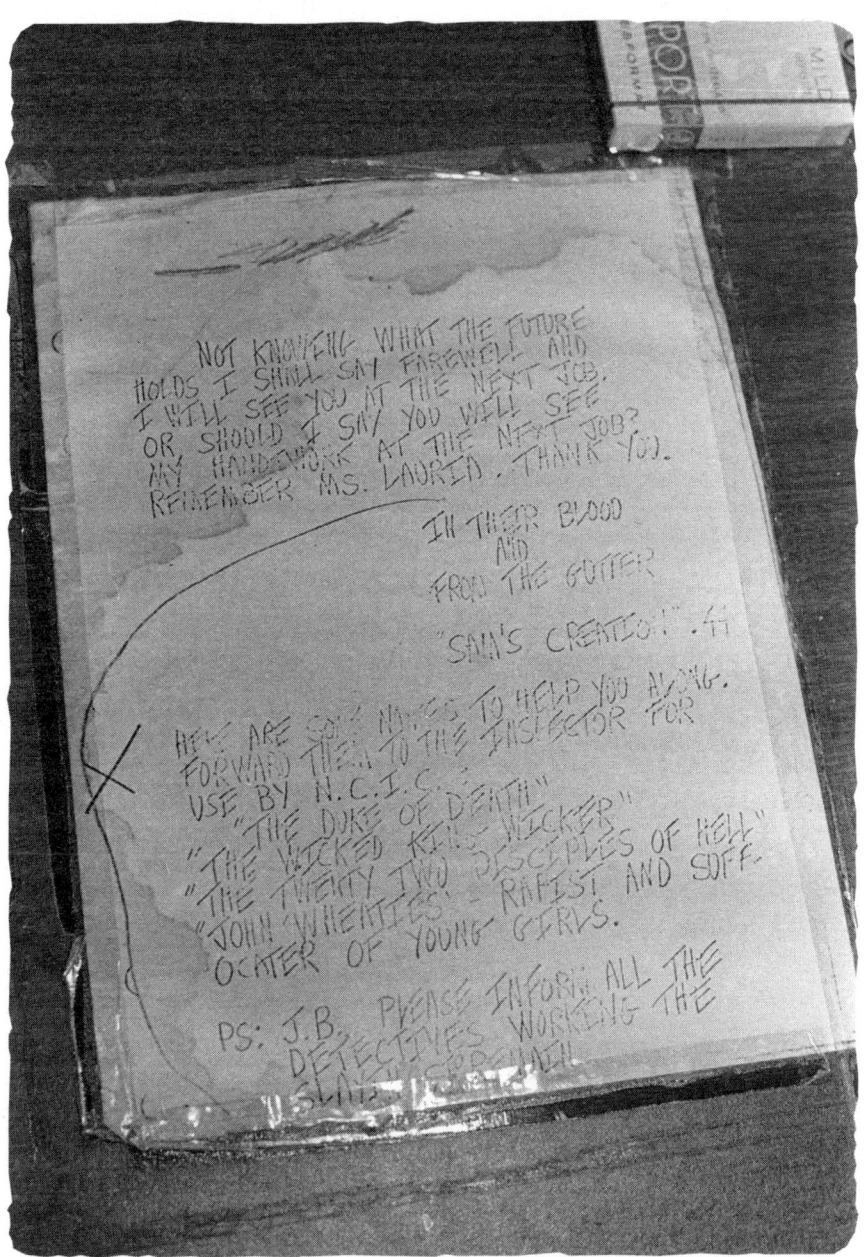

A letter sent to the journalists Jimmy Breslin and Dick Schaap from Berkowitz,
in his persona as the 'Son of Sam'.

Berkowitz did not write to Breslin again while he was at large. However, he did write to his former landlord in New Rochelle, Jack Cassara, who was the General Cosmo of his fantasies.

'I understood he had fallen off the roof of his house,' said Berkowitz. 'I was happy and sad when I heard about it. I had mixed emotions when I wrote to him.'

How did he hear Cassara had fallen off the roof?

'This demon dog told me. That's how I knew.'

In fact, Cassara had not fallen off the roof. Nevertheless, on 10 June he got a letter. It read,

Dear Jack,

I'm sorry to hear about that fall you took from the roof of your house. JUST WANT TO SAY 'I'M SORRY'. BUT I'M SURE IT WON'T BE LONG UNTIL YOU FEEL MUCH BETTER, HEALTHY, WELL AND STRONG.

Please be careful next time. Since your going to be confined for a long time, let us know if Nann needs anything.

Sincerely, Sam & Francis [sic]

The envelope also contained a get-well-soon card with a picture of a German shepherd dog on it and the return address on the envelope said Sam Carr, 316 Warburton Avenue, Yonkers.

Increasing madness

Cassara found Carr's number in the telephone directory, called him and they met up. Carr explained about the strange letters he had received, so Cassara contacted the police too.

In the discussion between the two families, the name of Berkowitz came up. By 6 August, Nann Cassara was convinced that Berkowitz was the Son of Sam.

Deputy Sheriff Craig Glassman was another neighbour of Berkowitz who also received an anonymous letter. It said, 'I know the Cassaras and Carr are out to get me and they put you [Glassman] here.'

Berkowitz would walk around the apartment in stockinged feet.

'I was afraid master Craig might hear me and be angry,' he said.

He was a demon.

'He just came – he just appeared one day – this Craig. He remained hidden in the walls and in the floor. He made funny screams all night long. I used to beg him to stop yelling and screaming, but he'd never listen.'

Berkowitz began to write things about Glassman on the walls of his apartment:

As long as Craig Glassman is in the world, there will never be any peace, but there will be plenty of murders.

Craig Glassman worships the devil and has power over me.

My name is Craig Glassman and I shall never let a soul rest.

Glassman received two more threatening letters talking of 'the streets running red with blood at the judgement'. The author described himself as 'the slave'. Glassman was 'the master' or 'darling... [who] drove me into the night to do your bidding'.

Murderous excursion

In the heat of a New York summer, with the windows sealed with grey blankets, Berkowitz's shambolic studio apartment was a sweatbox. Occasionally, he would peep around the makeshift curtains at the Carrs' backyard.

'I was watching for movement,' he said. 'The demons wanted girls... Sugar and spice and everything nice. That's one of Sam's favourite sayings. Then they began to yell in the yard.'

Answering the call on 25 June, Berkowitz dressed and popped his .44 in a paper bag.

'I ran downstairs to my car. It was cooler in the early evening. The fresh air always seemed to clear my mind.'

He headed for Queens. Just before 3am, he drove past the Elephas discotheque in Bayside. Berkowitz parked a couple of blocks away, tucked his .44 in his waistband and walked towards the disco, following the cracks in the sidewalk.

Before he reached the club, he saw a couple sitting in a red Cadillac. One of them was a girl.

'I saw her long hair. I looked about. The street was deserted. I then began to approach the car from the rear, keeping just behind the right rear fender. When I reached the car's trunk, I stopped to get out the gun. Then I stepped onto the curb and took a few steps forward, which brought me out directly in front of the passenger's side. I could see them clearly in the front seat. The window was closed. They weren't looking in my direction. I crouched down to bring myself level with the girl, and I fired.'

Seventeen-year-old Judy Placido was hit in the right temple, the shoulder and the back of the neck. Twenty-year-old Salvatore Lupo was shot in the right forearm. Both survived, but were unable to give a description of their assailant.

Berkowitz ran back to his car and made off, passing a squad car coming the other way.

'The demons were protecting me,' he said. 'I had nothing to fear from the police.'

On 29 July 1977, the New York tabloids marked the anniversary of the death of Donna Lauria, the Son of Sam's first victim. There were fears that he might mark the anniversary with another killing.

The demons howl

Nothing happened on the 29th, but the following day Berkowitz headed for Queens. When the prospects there did not seem promising, he moved on to Huntington on Long Island.

'I purposely drove out to Long Island to kill someone. It didn't matter who I'd kill, whoever I'd come across. When I'd find the right one, I'd be told.'

When nothing happened, he turned west and headed for Brooklyn. He parked in Bay 17th Street next to a fire hydrant. As he walked away from his car, he noticed a police car stop.

'I watched them write a ticket,' he said.

Then he walked the streets. On Shore Road, the local lovers' lane, he spotted a young couple in a powder-blue Corvette under a streetlamp. He pulled the gun from his belt, but as he approached the car, the engine started.

'I wasn't sure that they had seen me. I couldn't move, so I just stood there waiting for someone to scream out at me. But nothing happened, only the car just began to move.'

He retreated into the city park across the street and stared back at the empty parking spot.

'I knew they had got me to this spot to kill. I couldn't understand why they let that couple get away. Maybe I was there to get someone else.'

A few minutes later, a 1969 Buick pulled into the parking spot beneath the streetlamp. Berkowitz watched as a young couple got out to take a stroll in the park.

'She looked at me, but did not say anything,' he said.

After taking a swing in the play area, they headed back and got into the car.

'I walked straight to the car. When I got to the rear of it, I looked around, then stepped onto the sidewalk. I moved right to the driver's side and pulled the gun out. The voices began again. They began to howl. I knew I'd have to go through with it this time. I didn't care if anyone saw me. It didn't matter, I had to shoot them.'

And so, he did.

'I shot the last three times at both of them. I really wanted the girl more than anything. I don't know why I shot the guy. But they were so close together.'

Twenty-year-old Stacy Moskowitz died of her injuries. Robert Violante, also 20, lost an eye.

This time, he had been spotted. Unconcerned, Berkowitz drove away.

'I kept on riding until I approached the Verrazano Narrows Bridge, and there I saw another park. I was now less than a mile from the shooting scene. It didn't matter because I was tired. I just parked my car. It was four thirty or so in the morning. I walked out to the park with the newspaper and found a bench. I sat on it for a long time. I sat there for the rest of the night. When the sun rose, I read the news.'

The following day, the *Daily News* carried the headline: '44-CAL KILLER SHOOTS 2 MORE Wounds B'klyn Couple in Car Despite Heavy Cop Dragnet.'

Final job

On the afternoon of 4 August, Berkowitz was out with his .44 again, but he left it under the front seat of his car when he went for a walk in Riverdale Park. Returning to his car, he drove past an apartment block in the Bronx where he had once lived.

'As soon as I got there, they started. It was terrible. I knew I'd never get away from them, and I drove away.'

Then he drove down Buhre Avenue, past Donna Lauria's apartment block where he had first killed.

'They promised me that I'd marry her,' he thought. 'But they lied. They always lied to me.'

By the end of July, Berkowitz had stopped calling his mother and half-sister Roz after they suggested he consult a psychiatrist. It wouldn't help, he said.

'Soon it would all be over. The end of the reign of terror was near,' he said later. 'Word was going out through the dogs about the final job... So, on the final assignment, I'd have to kill as many as I could, as quickly as possible. That would give the demons meat for a long spell.'

The venue for the final spree of mass murder had already been picked.

'The place where I'd been camping years before. Southampton. It was summer and there'd be lots of young people there. There'd be enough blood and flesh for them to last a while.'

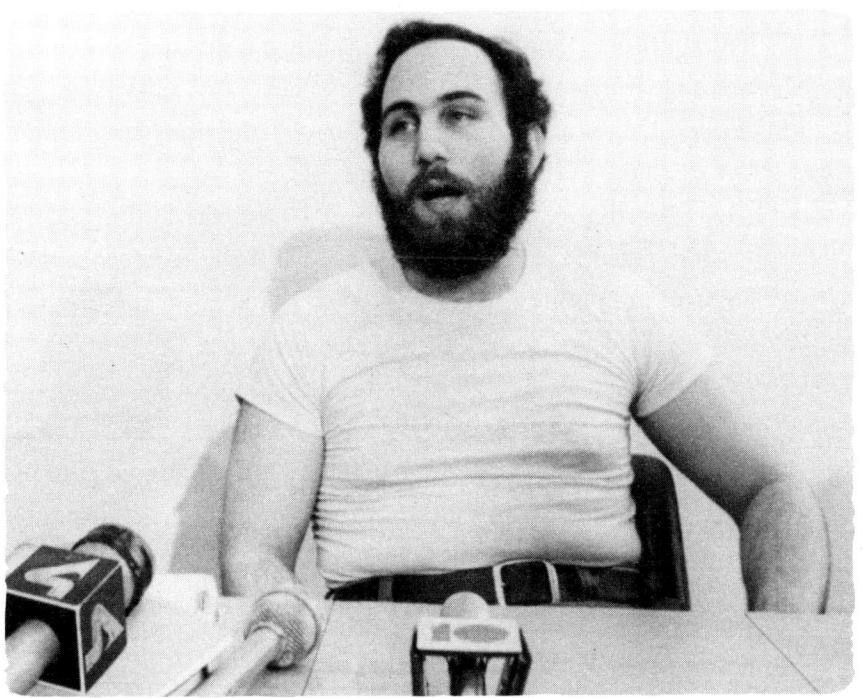

David Berkowitz gives a news conference from the Attica Correctional Facility in August 1980.

The net closes

On 6 August, Craig Glassman found a fire had been set outside his front door. When he doused it with a pot of water, he found .22 rifle cartridges among the ashes. The fire had not got hot enough to set them off.

The police connected the crazy letters that Glassman had received to those mailed to Sam Carr and Jack Cassara. The name David Berkowitz came up again.

By then, Berkowitz said he 'was getting tired of the whole thing'. That afternoon, he armed himself with his pistol and his semi-automatic rifle and drove out to the Hamptons. But by the time he reached Southampton, a thunderstorm had broken, courtesy of the demons. They did not want him to kill as many people as he wanted on his own initiative.

That afternoon, Sam Carr went to the police and told them he believed that Berkowitz was the Son of Sam. Two days later, the Yonkers Police Department called the Son-of-Sam task force, telling them about the letters Glassman had received.

'True, I am the killer,' said one, 'but Craig, the killings are at your command. I shall see you standing naked at the judgement seat...'

Checking the parking tickets issued in the area on the night of the Moskowitz–Violante shooting, the task force got the number of Berkowitz's car, which gave them his name and address.

On Wednesday 10 August 1977, Berkowitz packed his pump-action shotgun and three .22 rifles, including a semi-automatic, into his kit bag, along with enough ammunition to hold off an army and took them out to his car.

'Tonight, they'd have me go out again. This time, I'd take everything with me. I was ready...'

Meanwhile, homicide detective Eddie Zigo located Berkowitz's car and reported that he had found a machine gun on the back seat. Soon, the area was crawling with police.

No escape

It wasn't until 10pm that Berkowitz came out of his apartment block and walked over to his car carrying his .44 in a paper bag. He was approached by Detective John Falotico, who told him to freeze.

'Who are you?' asked Falotico.

'You know who I am,' said Berkowitz.

'No. You tell me who you are,' said Falotico.

'I'm Sam,' came the reply.

At police headquarters, Berkowitz admitted everything. He refused his lawyer's advice to plead not guilty by reason of insanity and, instead, pleaded guilty to eight shootings. At his sentencing hearing, he shouted, 'Stacy is a whore. I'd kill her again. I'd kill them all again.'

He was sentenced to 25 years to life for each murder to be served consecutively. Since his incarceration, Berkowitz has become an evangelical Christian, now styling himself Son of Hope rather than Son of Sam.

Otherwise, he claimed he had joined a Satanic cult in 1975 and had only killed three of the Son-of-Sam victims. There were also allegations that his putative cult had connections to Charles Manson.

CHAPTER EIGHT

Albert DeSalvo

To find fame as a serial killer, you need a good nickname. It started with Jack the Ripper. Then we had the Son of Sam, while Albert DeSalvo found fame as the Boston Strangler. He killed 13 women between 1962 and 1964 in and around Boston, Massachusetts. Most were sexually assaulted and strangled in their apartments.

DeSalvo was not even a suspect until he was arrested for rape in November 1964, then confessed all. His first victim as the Strangler was 55-year-old Latvian seamstress, Anna Elza Slesers, who he murdered in an apartment block on Gainsborough Street, Boston on 14 June 1962. His confession was matter of fact.

'I knocked on the door of Apartment 3F. A woman wearing a blue robe – I guess it was flannel – opened the door.

'"I came to work on the apartment," I said.

'We talked about the work and she let me in. As she walked and I was behind her, I hit her on the head with the lead weight. She fell. I reached over the back of her and I put my arms around her neck and we fell to the floor together…

'Her blood was all over me. I got up, took her robe… I had the robe belt, a blue one, and I put it around her neck and gave it two turns – tightened it good – and knotted it and I think it caught into a kind of bow, you understand? I left it on her.

'I think she was alive when I had intercourse with her. Then I washed up in the bathroom… I bundled up my bloody clothes and left.'

DeSalvo said that he felt an irresistible urge to kill.

'When this certain thing comes on me, it's a very immediate thing. I get up in the morning and I get this feeling and I tell my wife I'm going out on my job, but I'm not. I could always get out of the house because of my work and the kind of work I was doing – for a construction company – kept me out a lot anyway on the streets…'

DeSalvo did not look for a specific type of woman.

'What I had in mind was a picture of Woman, an image – not of anyone I knew, but just of all they had and what I needed to have the sex thing with them.'

But he did have a detailed memory of each incident.

Evil intruder

'That day was the first one – it was in summer, 1962 and I think it was raining or going to rain because I remember I had a raincoat with me – I told my wife I was going fishing and I took my rod and a fishing net that had these lead weights in it – it was out of the net that I got the weight I used on her… I must have known I was going to do it because I had the lead weight in my pocket when I went into her building.'

It was Number 77.

'I remember it said that on the glass over the door in gold letters. I went in and she let me in without no trouble… most of them was scared at first, but I talk good and act like I don't care whether they let me in or not. I talk fast and they ain't sure what I'm saying sometimes. I done it to hundreds of them. Just about every one of them let me in. I only had to slip a few locks and you know I been a B and E [breaking and entering] man a long time, so that don't give me no trouble to do that, but I don't need to do it most of the time with almost all the women I done things to.

'Inside her apartment, to the left, was the kitchen, then, down the little hall, maybe ten feet, the bathroom. The light was on. I see a sewing machine. It was brown. A window with drapes, a light-tan bedroom set, a couch, a record player, tan with dark-coloured knobs... the bathroom was yellow, the tub was white and she was going to take a bath because there was water in it... music is playing, long-hair symphonies and stuff like that... after, I turned it off, but I ain't sure I did get it all the way off.'

She took him to the bathroom to show him what work had to be done – making the mistake of turning her back on him.

'When I see the back of her head, I hit her on the head with the lead weight. She fell. I put my arms around her neck and we fell together on the floor. She bled a lot, terrible. While lying on the floor until she lay helplessly in my arms, the blood was going all over me... after I put the belt around her neck, I ripped open her robe and I played with her and I pulled her legs apart, like this, and I had intercourse... I think she was still alive when I had intercourse with her.'

But there was more than sex involved. He was angry and confused.

'Then I look around and I'm angry and I don't know why and I don't really know what I'm looking for.

'After, I took off my jacket and shirt and washed up and made a bundle. I grabbed her raincoat out of the brown cabinet in her bedroom... I see a 20-dollar bill on the cabinet shelf and I took it. That was the only money I took anyplace.

'I went out wearing her raincoat, a tan one, carrying my shirt and jacket wrapped in my own raincoat. The first thing I see when I come out of the building is a cop. He's walking by. He looks at me, but I don't pay no attention to him and go right past him to my car.'

Inside information

DeSalvo was then 32 and a former military policeman. At the time, he was a manual labourer, living with his wife and two children in the

Albert DeSalvo enters court, chained to another prisoner.

Boston suburb of Malden. He was being held in a mental hospital when his confession came to the ears of F Lee Bailey, one of the attorneys who later represented O J Simpson at his murder trial. What made DeSalvo all the more convincing was that he confessed to murders that were not on the official Strangler roster, such as that of 85-year-old Mary Mullen.

'I have told Mr Bailey that there was an old lady – I don't know her name – who is not considered one of the Strangler's women but who really is.

'She lived on Commonwealth Avenue and I caused her to die about two weeks after Anna Slesers... she died in my arms, this woman... this is too much, I'm getting sick, talking about it. She was so old, this woman, it is hard to believe that I did it to her, a woman in her late-seventies or her eighties.

'But that isn't all of it. You see, I have a special reason for not liking to talk about this one and it is not only because of what I made happen to her or because of anything that I did to her in the way of sex...'

That said, the assault itself was easy.

'It was all so simple and yet so much like a funny kind of dream – a nightmare – I walked up to the second floor of this building, and I knocked on the door of the first apartment I came to. This old lady opens it and I say that I got to work on the apartment and, as usual, she lets me in. I guess I look like a guy who works on apartments or something because they all fall for it – oh hundreds of them, hundreds – and it got so that I could score a piece of ass on a 20-minute trip into Boston and be headed back home very close to my usual time so as not to get Irmgard, my wife, asking questions...'

Mrs Mullen was a kindly old lady and she wasn't suspicious at all.

'She let me in right away and she invited me to sit down and tell her what I was supposed to be doing for work on the place. She was so trusting and she treated me right, I can't understand... The whole thing on this one bothers me. It's like a nightmare, a double nightmare, going back like this. She looked like my grandmother... I got behind her when she turned. I don't know what happened... all I know is that my arm went around her neck.'

She was old, weak and defenceless.

'I wouldn't of had to squeeze at all, but as it turned out she just went straight down, so suddenly terrified, I guess. I didn't want to see her fall on the floor, so I tried to hold her, but she sort of sank right down to the floor. I think she was dead then. I think she died in my arms when she realized who I was or what I was doing; it was a shock she just couldn't take...'

Until DeSalvo's confession, Mary Mullen's death had been ascribed to natural causes.

Double killing

Two days later, on 30 June 1962, DeSalvo committed two murders.

'This day I went to Salem and I rode around for a while and I ended up in Lynn... sometimes, I'm driving to work and building the image up and then I get release right in my underwear, but five minutes later I'm ready again and the image comes back and the pressure mounts up into my head.'

In Lynn, he stopped in front of 72 Newhall Street, waiting around a while before starting up the back stairs, but someone was coming, so he went back to the front door, climbed the stairs to the second floor and knocked on a door.

'I never been in this building before, I don't know nobody here, this woman, I don't know her. I don't know who lives in the apartment, whether or not it is a woman, but I knock and I know what I'll say when she opens the door, I don't think about it, I just know, see?'

He said he had come to do some work on the apartment, but the woman said it was the first she had heard of it.

'"Well, lady, I'm telling you about it now," I say, smiling and looking down like I don't want to look at her standing there in her pyjamas with the door cracked open five or six inches. "I don't want to bother you," I say, taking a step away, that's always a good one and it usually works – you are saying, I don't give a damn whether you let me in or not. I say, "I really don't want to bother you and if I ain't done the work that ain't my fault but yours, so you can't complain to the super, okay, lady?"

"'Well,' she says, opening the door a little more. "It just seems funny that I never heard of it is all."

"'I'm supposed to check the windows for leaks, too," I say and that one got her…

"'Well, it's about time," she said, "but I still don't know you."

'The door is opened a little more… so help me, this thing going in my head, this pressure, I want to say, don't open the door, but I still want it to open, it's funny, you know?'

Mad with rage

By then, the door was open pretty wide and she was standing in it in her cotton pyjamas.

'So help me, now I'm hoping she'll not let me in to do it to her and at the same time going on making her let me as if I couldn't stop the con I'm giving her… The thing is, she never done nothing to me and I am going to do something to her. I don't know why, and she don't know me and I don't know her.

'So anyway, she let me in and then it had to happen…'

They went through into the bedroom.

'When she turned her back, I put my arms around her neck and she went into a dead faint. A little blood was coming from her nose. She was a heavy-set, big-breasted woman, very well built.

'I picked her up and took her pyjamas off. I took everything off and got on top of her. She was alive, but unconscious. I remember biting her bust and other parts of her body too… I put the bra around her neck… a nylon stocking, too…

'I think she was dead then and I could see the blood, just a little, coming from her nose, and the red marks of the bites on her big breasts and down her belly almost to the – what is the polite word for her privates? – almost to the hair of that… I remember she had a big bush and for an old lady she was very well built…'

Again, he was angry and confused.

'It made me mad, somehow, to see her like that, dead, and with come on her hair and I gave the stuff around her neck a good turn and then I went through her place, but I didn't take nothing… I don't know what I was looking for and I am very angry and I don't know what about.'

The victim was 65-year-old nurse Helen Blake. When the neighbours did not see her all day, they got the key off the superintendent of the building, then they called the police. That was around 5pm. An hour later, DeSalvo was ringing the doorbell of 68-year-old physiotherapist, Nina Nichols.

'I been riding around all day like in the middle of the world, and I got to this parking lot down on Commonwealth Avenue and I left my car there and walked to Number 1940.

'I look at the names on the mailboxes and the bells inside Number 1940 and pick out a couple of names and press the first one.'

Nothing happened, so he pressed the second doorbell. After a few minutes, the door buzzed, twice, and he walked into the hallway.

'It's funny, ain't it, how the first woman didn't answer the bell or wasn't home or something and just that little chance [changed everything]…'

Same old con

Once more, it would be easy pickings.

'She had on a robe, you might say a housecoat… and I remember she had glasses on.'

She asked what he wanted.

'She sounded kind of mad, like impatient, as if I was a bother to her.'

He used the maintenance man con again.

'I said, "We been wanting to check your apartment windows for leaks." It always came to me what to say and it was always something simple and easy.'

He said that the building superintendent had sent him. If she did not believe him, she should call him up.

'And she said, "Oh, all right, come in, make it fast. I'm just getting ready to go out."

'But I already know that she ain't going nowhere after I close that door behind me, even though I fight it all the way. It's funny, I didn't want to go in there in the first place. I just didn't want it to happen…'

They went from one room to another. Then, in the bedroom, she turned her back on him.

'I see the back of her head, and – I was all hot, just like my head was going to blow off as soon as I saw the back of her…

'I grabbed her and she fell back with me on the bed, on top of me. She was digging her nails into my hands and I recall her drawing blood.'

He was reluctant to say what happened next – 'the thing with the bottle'.

'She was still conscious, and I took her off the bed and I lied her on the floor and I opened her housecoat, tearing some of the buttons. She was wearing something underneath – it was just a slip and I lifted it up above her waist and I had intercourse with her there on the floor… all that stuff in my head went out with the come like a dam got opened and for a minute I felt good and then I looked at her and she still looked alive, and so I went and got two nylon stockings… I put a silk stocking around her neck and knotted it tight, three times, like this…

'All the time, the thing is building up in me again and I am getting mad, very angry… so I take another silk stocking and put it around her neck. It was only later when I got over being mad that I came back and made the big bows in the ends of the stockings, fixing them in big loops, so that they look pretty, like a decoration... but that was later, right then, when I strangled her with the stockings, I was very, very angry at her. I don't how her and she never done nothing to me, but I'm very angry and pull them stockings awful tight.'

Then he got up and went through the place.

'I don't know what I'm looking for and that makes me madder, and so that is when I went back and got the bottle... I want to tell you about that bottle, sir. It was not the first time that I used something on a woman.

'Some of the other women liked it and said for me to come back and do it to them again. But I think this woman was dead... now this bottle it was a wine bottle, I would say... I recall taking a bottle some time after I got off her... there might have been wine in the bottle... it was green. I stuck the bottle in her vagina hole.

'I stuck the end of that wine bottle into her and pushed it until it would not go in more and her vagina was spread pretty far and I kept pushing... until it was way up there and just wouldn't go no more.'

He said he didn't like to talk about it.

'When you ask me why I did it, I can't tell you. For what reason I don't know, I stuck the bottle in her. I think I left it in her. These things, I'm ashamed of what I done.... Why I done it, I don't really understand...'

Then he began to bite her.

'I bit her on the breasts. Why I did this, I don't know, but it was not to draw blood. That is not what I did it for, but I bit her several times on the breasts, enough to leave the marks of my teeth, and why I had to do that I couldn't tell you...'

The phone started ringing and he fled the apartment.

'I look back just before I open the door and I see her there with her legs open and that bottle...

'There's a noise down at the bottom of the stairs, the elevator comes up and stops on a floor just below. I can just see that it's a woman getting off and going down the hall and I hear her keys clink and a door open and close... then I go down the stairs and go to my car in the parking lot... I got into the car and drove out, turning into Commonwealth Avenue and out to where I could pick up Route 3, which would take me home to Malden. It was coming close to six o'clock.'

The victim, 68-year-old Nina Nicholas, had been on the phone to her sister when the doorbell rang and said she would call back. When she did not, her sister called her. There was no answer. Her sister's husband eventually called the super, who entered using the pass key, found Nina's body and called the police.

Too trusting

Next, just a few weeks later, on 19 August, he killed 75-year-old Edes 'Ida' Irga.

'I was driving around like always when the thing was on me. I didn't pick her out in advance. I didn't know the building. There was a parking place on Grove Street and that was how it happened. There was a parking place in front of her building. If there was no parking place, I'd never of got her. I just happened to walk into her building at 7 Grove Street.

'Now, let me say this, sir. I know that at the time everybody was scared of the Strangler... everybody was supposed to be looking out for themselves – especially women living alone – but I tell you right now that it never was no trouble to get in anywhere. If they had, they might be alive.'

He rang four different bells in the hall downstairs before someone pressed the buzzer. Ida asked what he wanted and he said he had come to do some work, even though it was Sunday night.

'I tell you this because there was so much made of how the Strangler got into them places without forcing a lock or anything like that...'

Again, the victim was old and not likely to put up much of a fight.

'I remember what she looked like, but I can't remember what she was wearing. She was short and heavy and an old lady, very homely-looking, too. No, not attractive, as you say, but attractiveness had nothing to do with it – she was a woman.'

Looking past her, he could see that the ceiling needed some work, so she let him in.

'We went into the bedroom, where I was supposed to look for more work. I asked her to check behind the curtains of the windows for leaks and, when she turned, I put my arm around her back and got her by the neck and strangled her manually.'

She passed out fast.

'I saw purplish-dark blood, it came out of her right ear. I saw it more clearly when I put the pillowcase around her neck… but I strangled her first with my arm, then the pillowcase. I think I had intercourse with her then. To me, it's sickening even to talk about this. It's so damn real – that blood coming out of her ear.'

But that did not stop him.

'While she lay on the floor in the bedroom, I torn her dress open and pulled off everything she had on under it – which was not very much – and she had a withered pair of breasts, which was heavy and not soft or smooth and – during the intercourse I had with her – yes, I did bite them and leave some marks and I did bite the rolls of fat in her belly and it is true that also I did not just insert my own penis but other objects into her…

'Then I threw things around and I dragged her out into the other room and I took two chairs and put her legs in a wide position, with the feet on the chairs, wide apart… then I had to masturbate and I let the come out on the rug near her.'

Killing for thrills

Although the media had used the term 'Strangler', the police refused to confirm that a serial killer was at large, claiming that each murder had been committed by a separate killer. It made no difference to DeSalvo.

'The very next day, the thing was on me again. I drove and drove, in and out and around. I wound up in Dorchester at this building… There's a lot of doorbells and mailboxes. I see some women's names, I don't know them. I never been to this place before. I ring and almost right away somebody buzzes, so I get in easy.

'Inside, there are stairs, but her apartment was on the first floor. I knock. She wouldn't even open it, she was so scared, but she says from behind the closed door, "What is it?" and I said that I was sent by the super and she wanted to know what for and I said, well, if we're going to talk, can't she open the door and she says that she's scared and very nervous. I said, "Then never mind, I'll come back later." She opened the door then.'

But she kept it on the chain, opening it only about five or six inches.

'I could see that she was very, very nervous and scared. I looked past her into the apartment – if I can see something, anything, I know that I can talk my way in. I see right off that she's moving in because she's setting things up.'

It wasn't as easy as before, but he kept talking fast.

'I told her I was there to do some work, finish off the apartment for her. She was very, very nervous. I talked so fast she thought I came either from the landlord or the movers. She let me in.

'She took me in, room to room, and I said they didn't do a good job here and she said yes, they left a mess. I said yes, but first I had to look everything over… I got her right next to the bathroom, when she was coming out of the room she turned her back to me. I grabbed her and we fell together.'

This time, the victim put up a fight.

'Boy, that woman struggled! She almost made it. I put my right arm around her and wrapped my legs around hers, but she was big and hard to hold and very strong. She almost got away. I couldn't hold her... a very strong woman. Another second and she was free. But she passed out.

'She was an older woman, but very solidly built. I had sex with her right there on the floor.

'When I finished, I looked at her. She was nearly naked and her body was very solid. She was breathing, but still, unconscious – and for some reason, she made me angry, seeing her like that, this woman, and I went and got a broomstick from the kitchen and I did things to her with the broomstick... I took the broom, I put the broom up there. Then, I went and got something and put it around her throat. I would say it was a couple of nylon stockings. I tied them around her neck...

'I went into the bathroom and turned the water on in the tub. I went back and picked her up. She was a heavy woman... I remember pushing her, so that she sunk in the water.'

The victim was 67-year-old nurse, Jane Sullivan. Her body was found ten days later by her nephew.

The Measuring Man

DeSalvo then took a few months off, but the urge to kill did not go away.

'It was on me again, the urge, the thing. It never stopped, but why I had to kill sometimes, I don't understand... it always happened for what, to me, seems no good reason... I never knew for sure what it would be or why those women were picked out... I didn't know them and they never done nothing to me...'

He remembered when the next attack took place because it was 5 December, his wedding anniversary, and he had taken the day off. Nevertheless, 'I knew I had to go looking for the satisfaction, for Woman,' so he told Irmgard that he had a little work to do in the afternoon, took the car and drove around.

'I parked my car on Huntington Avenue. It was some time after two o'clock. The street and sidewalk was slushy and the wind was blowing sharp and cold. I walked to Number 315 Huntington.

'The downstairs door was open, so I went on up to Apartment 4C. I knocked and the girl who came to the door was Sophie Clark.'

This time the victim was young and attractive.

'I will describe her as she presented herself to me... a Negro girl, beautiful, with beautiful long hair. Her eyes were dark brown. She looked like a Hawaiian girl – dark-skinned and with that long, beautiful hair. She was tall. Five-ten, which is taller than me. She was built solid, too, at least one hundred and forty pounds. She had on a sexy, whitish-type robe... she had black high heels on, I remember, and black stockings...'

He said he had some repair work to do on the apartment and she said she couldn't let anybody in because her roommates weren't there.

'She seemed to realize that this was not a smart thing to say, and added, "My roommates are just across the street in the YMCA, they are taking a course there, they'll be back any minute, I'm waiting for them."'

He could see that she was scared, so he kept talking and finally she let him into the apartment.

'When I got inside, I stood talking with her in the little hallway, leaning against the wall, and I brought the subject around to my old measuring bit.'

Before DeSalvo started killing, he had been the 'Measuring Man'. He would approach young women in their homes, saying he was looking for potential models. He would ask to take their measurements. This gave him the opportunity to touch them, sometimes inappropriately. Some would be persuaded to strip. This led to consensual sex, or indecent assault, then rape.

'"You know something, Sophie," I said, "your roommates, Audri and Gloria, have often said to me how well you are built – you know something, you could be a model with a figure like yours."'

He pretended he knew her roommates and had got their names from the card beside the bell in the foyer downstairs.

"'Oh, they are just talking," Sophie said, but I could see that she was flattered.

"'No, they're not just talking, Sophie," I said, "I know, because I've done some work in the modelling field – setting girls up in it.'"

It was his old Measuring Man con.

Fatal mistake

"'Do you know your actual measurements?" She said she didn't and I said, "Please turn around and let me see how you are built..."

'She turned and that was it. I grabbed her around the neck with my right arm. She fell back on top of me. She couldn't talk and she was having a hard time breathing. She was weak, I suppose, from being scared when now she knew who I was...'

She passed out.

'I had intercourse with her... she was having her period and I had to take off her sanitary napkin... I had intercourse with her and she was still unconscious. I did not undress her before I had intercourse with her, I did that later...'

When he saw she was coming to, he grabbed two nylon stockings out of a drawer.

'I began to tie the nylons around her neck. She came to a little and she was putting up a fight now. I stuck a gag into her mouth. Now, she was looking at me, right at me, and I had the nylons around her neck, but she kept struggling, so I had to pull them tight... so tight I couldn't see it. I ripped off her slip and put it around her neck, then I took an elastic belt and put that around her neck, too... and I think that is when she died...'

He felt remorseful.

'There was no need for it to happen. She wasn't a tramp, but a good person. There was no reason for her to die...'

But that did not stop him.

'I did things to her. I remember an icetray… I don't know why I did that… I remember spreading her legs wide open and that she looked wild and sexy with her garter belt still holding up her black stockings and her legs spread wide like that. I masturbated and came on the rug beside her body.

'It was over in a short time… It was just about three o'clock when I left.'

Roommates Audri and Gloria returned at 5.30pm to find 20-year-old Sophie dead.

Breaking and entering

After Christmas, he attacked again in nearby Park Drive.

'It was about 10.30 on Sunday morning, December 30th… about three weeks after Sophie Clark… I was not there on a sex thing especially. I was thinking of pulling a B and E.'

So, he slipped the lock and got in that way.

'When I opened the door, somebody says from the other room, "Who is that? Who is there?"

'For a minute, I was surprised, then I said, "It's me, Al Johnson, from upstairs, who is that?"

'"It's Pat," she said. "What do you want?"'

He said he had come to see one of her roommates. She said there was no one there but her.

'She had brown hair, very soft and nice, cut kind of short, and she had very pretty blue eyes. She was dressed in a robe, with some kind of pyjamas showing under it… sexy, leopardlike pyjamas. She was not a beautiful girl in the face, but she was very well built and she was kind of pretty.

'"So you are one of the fellows from upstairs," she said. I could see that she was a friendly person.

'She was very nice to me, she treated me like a man – I thought of doing it to her and I talked myself out of it. I wanted to get out of there, you know… so I said, standing up, "Well, I've got to go, tell your friend that I was by, will you?"'

Despite his misgivings, the die was cast.

'She was too friendly, you might say that she almost did it to herself. "Oh, wait and have some coffee," she said, "I'll put some on."

'I still wanted to get out, even then. "I'll go and get some doughnuts," I said.

'"No need to go out," she said. "I've got something we can have."

'Then it was as good as over. I didn't want it to happen, but then I knew that it would.'

They sat in the kitchen for a while and talked.

'I am too excited to touch my coffee, then I say, "You got a nice figure, Pat. I'd like to measure it to find out if you could be a model." She laughs and says, "All you guys upstairs got these lines?"

'Then I get up, I really want to get out of there and don't want to do anything to her. She has been very nice to me and I don't want to hurt her, but I can feel the urge on me. She says, "Oh, come on in the living room and we can talk some more."'

By that time, DeSalvo said, it had gotten beyond his ability to control.

'There is nothing that I can do about it by that time I go into the living room with her. She put on a Christmas record and was talking about innocent things, but I was looking at her and getting worked up. I went over to her. I get down on my knees and take her by the ankles. I say, "I'd like to measure you, Pat."

'All that she says is: "Hey, listen, Al, take it easy, will you?"

'But I am gone at this point, beyond stopping me. I know it, but it is sad for her. It is too bad, but it can't be helped.'

And he got aggressive.

'"Look," I say, "I got my hands on your ankles, I could go all the way up if I want to. Who is going to stop me? Nobody's here. Nobody could stop me, nobody could hear you if you yelled. I can do what I want with you."

'She grew angry. "If that is the way you are going to talk," she said, "you'd better go right now. I don't want people around who are going to be like that."

'She turned her back on me... next thing, before she knew it, I had my arm around her neck from in back. She fell back on top of me.'

She had passed out.

'I put her on the bed and I looked at her. Naturally, when I saw her, the sex thing come on strong. I opened her robe. Underneath, she had on these sexy leopardlike pyjamas. I ripped them off... I wanted to see her busts... that is to say that her leopard pyjamas was ripped off or pulled away from her busts and her privates, up over her busts and down around her ankles.

'I had intercourse with her while she was unconscious, but still alive... She had treated me right and here I was doing this thing to her which she didn't want me to do. I am sorry about that one, really sorry, but she shouldn't of asked me to stay...'

Why did he do it?

While again blaming his victim for what had happened to them, he was confused about his motives once more.

'I don't know if I done this for a sex act or for hatred or for what reason... all I can say is that, when I saw her body, the sex act came in. I did not enjoy the sexual relations with this woman. I was thinking too much about that she would not have wanted to do it. There was no thrill at all.

'There was some nylon stockings hanging up there. I took one of them and I took a blouse and I tied them tight around her throat... tight... oh, when I was doing it, I was saying why am I doing it to her? What has she done to me? And there was no answer then... no answer now... At the end, I covered her up.'

Then, there was the remorse.

'She was not like most of them, she was so different... I didn't want anyone to see her like that, naked and without anything... I can remember that I was pulling those things tight around her neck and she couldn't breathe and how her face was swelling up... her face getting bigger, redder, like it was going to explode... I don't know why I did it. She did me no harm. Why did I do it to her? She treated me like a man.'

The body of 23-year-old Patricia Jane Bissette was found when her boss stopped by the following day to give her a lift to work. When

Eight of DeSalvo's victims (from top left to bottom right): Rachel Lazarus, Helen E. Blake, Ida Irga, Mrs J. Delaney, Patricia Bissette, Daniela M. Saunders, Mary A. Sullivan, Mrs Israel Goldberg. There is no discernible type. He just wanted to kill 'Woman' and he did not know why.

he could not rouse her, he got the building superintendent to enter her apartment.

More lies

On 18 February 1963, DeSalvo attacked a young German immigrant named Gertrude Gruen. She fought back, biting his finger through to the bone. He fled.

'Why I did not kill that girl, I don't know,' he said. 'I certainly could have, but something made me stop. I don't know what it was.'

The police were convinced that this was an abortive attempt by the Strangler, but Gertrude Gruen was so traumatized that she could not give any usable description.

Then on 9 March 1963, it happened again. 'It was about ten in the morning. I had been driving all around and now I find myself in Lawrence… this day, as I walk into this building, I see a nine-inch brass pipe, about an inch-and-a-half thick, behind the door of the vestibule. I pick it up. I don't know why.

'I stand there a minute, looking at names on the wall beside the bells. I see this name Mary Brown… Mrs Mary Brown… I knock on her door. I got the pipe in my back pocket. She comes to the door and she is an older woman. I would say in her sixties.'

He told her he had come to paint the kitchen.

'She said, "This isn't giving much notice, is it?"

'I say, "Don't worry about it. I'll help you clear the kitchen out. "As she walked to the kitchen, her back was to me. I hit her right on the back of the head with the pipe. She went down.

'Now, this was terrible, and I don't like talking about it… she went and I ripped her things open, showing her busts… she was unconscious and bleeding… I don't know why, but then I hit her again on the head with the pipe. I kept on hitting and hitting her with the pipe… this is unbelievable… oh, it was terrible… because her head felt like it was all gone… then I took this fork and stuck it into her right bust and I left it there… I covered her with a sheet… it was bloody… oh, wasn't it, my God!'

The police did not immediately ascribe the murder of 69-year-old Mary Ann Brown to the Strangler. Some had their suspicions because of the way her body had been hastily stripped, but it was only when DeSalvo confessed that she was added to the official list of victims.

DeSalvo was said to have wept when he related the details of the murder of Mrs Brown. But the next murder two months later was just as ferocious.

Almost too easy

'At 8.30am, Monday, May 6, 1963, I was on my way to work and the thing come on me. I shot over to Cambridge, just random, because, as I have said, it often took me less than 20 minutes to score a piece of ass and get out… you would be surprised how easy it is to do nowadays when these girls got the pill and they don't really give a goddam how it, sex, is given out… this is especially true of Cambridge.

'So I go, just random, I hit an apartment house. It looks familiar and I say to myself, yes, I been there before as the Measuring Man. That don't stop me. I got nothing but contempt for these broads who ain't bright enough to know what the hell I am doing… all they have to do is to ask me a couple of simple questions and I am done.'

By this time, it was well known that a serial killer was on the prowl, but still DeSalvo found it almost too easy.

'I go to this place anyway and I go into the vestibule and pick out a name at random… I press the bell and pretty soon the buzzer goes. Sometimes I say to myself, "Why do they press the buzzer?" They don't know who is down there ringing the bell… and these days, it could be the Boston Strangler. But anyway, the buzzer goes and I am in.'

He went up to the second floor, found the apartment and knocked on the door. A young woman answered the door and he said he had come to do some work on the apartment.

'She is not the prettiest girl I ever see. She's got a nice face, but it seemed to me that her chin is too big, but she is still a very attractive girl, if that is what you are looking for – which I am not. I am looking for Woman – and she got all the things that I build up in my mind and call by that name – so that if she invites me in, I am going to make her give me what I want.'

He had with him a jack-knife with a blade 4–4.5 in (10–11.5 cm) long.

'She says, well, all right you can come in, but where are your tools? And I say, "First we got to see what the work is to be done before we go lugging tools around." She says, "Yes, that makes sense."

'To tell you the truth, I had had it with this girl. She was too clever, too tight, and what she had, goddamn it, I could get somewhere else, you know – what is it, really, but the little fur between the legs and those tits to fool around with? No matter how homely or old a woman is, she still got these, see. This broad seemed to me like a Sunday-school girl. But anyway, for one reason or another, I don't know why, really, she let me in. She says, "Oh, well, come in and get it over with." That is exactly what I do.'

Sex at knifepoint

As soon as he was in and closed the door behind him, he brought the knife out of his pocket and opened it.

'She says, "What is this for?" And I say, "If you don't scream, I won't hurt you." She says, "What is it you want?" And I say, "I just want to make love to you." She says, right off, "I won't let you – that is not a nice thing to do." Oh, why didn't I get out of there right off? I should have heard what she was saying… but I didn't hear it, really, although it was an echo, an exact echo of what I had been hearing for a long time from Irmgard…

'So anyway, I say to her, all right, so I won't make love to you. I'll just play around with you. She says, "But look, promise me that you won't make me pregnant." I never met a broad like that before, I mean one who is willing to let you do just about what you want as long as you don't get her pregnant, you know?

'What could you say to a woman like that? I said, "No, just fool around with you and leave."'

He told her to lie down on the bed and she asked him what he was going to do.

'I said, "I am going to tie you up and get some kicks out of you."

'She said, "Are you the Boston Strangler?"

'I said, "Yes, I am."

'I think that she passed out then. While she was unconscious, I stripped her and got her ready to do what I had to do.

'She came around just before I am ready to go. I been looking at her body and the bush at her crotch and the big tits and I am getting hotter than hell, even though she doesn't show any signs of life. I am thinking, what a goddamn shame that a broad with a body like this has to be so prudish when she has got all this to offer a man...'

He preferred his victim to be inert.

'I tie her down and put a gag in her mouth, then she spit that gag out and I think that maybe I just put something over her head, so that she won't see me while I am doing it to her... I tied a cloth around her head over her mouth, so that she couldn't scream but would still be able to talk...

'I have her on the bed and she is naked, practically, and I look at her body... I played with her and I know that I am going to have intercourse with her anyway, no matter what she says about it.

'My head was ready to burst and everything was built up in me... but when she come to, she begin to talk and plead with me... "You promised," she says. "You said you wouldn't do it to me. Don't ... don't..."'

But things were only going to get worse.

'Then she begin to say things that make me feel unclean: "You are not a man, you are some kind of an animal... that is not nice...

why do you want to do things like that?… why are you kissing me on that?… you are not a man, you are an animal…"'

Frenzy of violence

'This woman make me feel unclean just like Irmgard, the way she talk with me.

'I had put the knife on the edge of the coffee table. I took it again and stabbed her in the throat. Once I stabbed her once, I couldn't stop. I grabbed the knife in my left hand and held the tip of her breast and went down two times, hard. She don't say anything now, she moved and the blood came, blood all over the place… I kept hitting her and hitting her with that knife… she kept bleeding from the throat… I hit her and hit her and hit her.'

The victim, Beverley Samans, was a 23-year-old graduate student at Boston University, who had had an audition for the Metropolitan Opera Company in New York that summer. Her body was discovered three days later by a boyfriend who had got the key from the super when Beverley did not answer the phone or a ring on her doorbell. She had been stabbed 22 times. The Strangler had left his signature nylon stockings tied around her neck.

Getting ready for church

A stocking was found tied around the neck of 57-year-old Marie Evelina 'Evelyn' Corbin on 8 September 1963. Another was tied around her ankle in an elaborate bow. Like the others, she was nearly nude.

'I got over to Salem that morning with this urge on,' said DeSalvo, 'and I didn't know where I was going. I stopped near this apartment house – I don't recall the street or number of that, but I know that her apartment was Number 3, I remember that. I go into the vestibule and look for women's names and I ring several bells. The buzzer goes and I go into the building. I remember that Number 3 had a woman's name on it, so I look for that. I knock.

'A woman's voice says, through the door, "Who is it?" I say that I'm from the super and that I got work to do in the apartment and she says, "Look, can't you come back later? I'm just getting ready for church." I say no, that I can only work now, since I got a full-time job and am only helping the super out.'

After a minute, she opened the door.

'"It's a funny time to come around to do work," she says, but I can see that she is going to let me in.

'"I'm sorry to be so suspicious," she said. "You never know who is knocking on your door these days." Then she said, in a joking way, "How do I know that you are not the Boston Strangler?"'

He said he would leave if she wanted him to, but she told him to hurry up because she didn't have much time.

'We went in and she went into the bathroom with me and right there I put the knife on her.

'"Keep quiet," I said, "and I won't hurt you."

'"What do you want?" she asked.

'"I just want to have intercourse with you," I said.

'"I can't do that," she said. "I was told by my doctor not to do it. I am not well."

'"All right, then," I said. "Will you blow me?"

'She began to cry, but she said that she would. I sat on the edge of the bed and she put a pillow on the floor and kneeled there and did it.'

But that was not going to be enough.

'When she got up and put the pillow back, I grabbed her by the robe. She turned around and the buttons popped off... the robe tore and under it she had a nightgown on and that tore, too, and her left breast showed.

'The next thing I know, I was strangling her. I strangled her manually. I put her on the bed. She was not dead yet. I got on top of her, sitting on her hands. I put the pillow on top of her face, so that I wouldn't have to look at her face. Then, I held onto her throat until she was dead.'

After that, he went around the place and found what he was looking for.

'I came back to her with two nylons. I put them around her neck and tied them, then I rip open her clothes and spread her legs as wide as I could. I went and got another nylon stocking and tied it around her ankle. I don't know why I did that. Then, I left and I don't think anyone saw me.'

Her body was discovered by a friend who had a spare key after Mrs Corbin failed to turn up for a lunch appointment.

Back in the headlines

On 22 November 1963, the Boston Strangler was ousted from the headlines by the assassination of President John F. Kennedy. But only for a day.

'I cried when Kennedy died… the next day, I went to Lawrence, to Joanne Graff's death,' said DeSalvo. He spotted her name on the letterbox in the hall downstairs.

'I don't know who she is or what she looks like. I was looking for a girl's name and it was the only one there.'

He went to the door of her apartment and knocked. She opened it a little. He said that the super had sent him to see what needed doing in the apartment. She said all right if it would only take a few minutes because she was getting ready to go out.

'The minute I see the apartment, I know that I had said the right thing. It needed work, all right.

'"I better check the bathroom," I said. "You show me what you want done in there."

'I could see that she was afraid to go into the bathroom with me since she was only dressed in a robe and what looked like black leotards.'

He told her that, if she did not show him what had to be done, she couldn't complain later.

'She was a timid girl, I could see that. She was used to doing what she was told, though, and she went into the bathroom and began looking around.

'I went right in after her. I could feel the heat in me and my head felt the pressure like pounding in it as if it was going to burst.

'When she sees me coming in, she looked like she was going to run out. But I had her cornered. She knew it and she stopped. I don't know what she was thinking.'

He pulled the knife on her. 'Don't scream, I won't hurt you,' he said.

'She just stood there. She was petrified. She couldn't have screamed if she had wanted to.

'"Now," I said. "Walk over to the bed."

'She walked past me and out into the room. She stopped at the bed. She still hadn't said a word. Her face, I recall, was very white.'

Someone walked by in the hall outside. He held his finger to his lips and threatened her with the knife.

'She understood and didn't try nothing.'

He went over to the door and listened, then went back to her.

'At that point, she tried to get away from me and I put my arm around her neck, and I pulled her back onto the bed. We fell back on the bed. She was on top of me, and she passed out.

'I ripped her blouse off. She was wearing leotards, black ones, and white shoes. I ripped the leotards off and they went around her neck.

'I stripped her almost naked. She had a beautiful body. Her busts were large, 38, very smooth, hefty. I played with her busts, I may have bitten them... yes, I think I did... I possibly may have bit her somewhere else on her body.

'She was unconscious, and I had intercourse with her.'

Afterwards, she began to come to.

'She opened her eyes and looked at me. "I am going to tie you up," I said.

'She said, "What have you done to me?"

'I said that all I had done was make love to her and she cried.

'I began to tie her up and she said, "Don't tie me up, please don't tie my hands, don't tie me…"

'I said that I couldn't leave her loose, that I had to get away, I had to have time to do that, that I would tie her in a way that she could easily get out of in a few minutes.

'But she wouldn't let me do it. She wanted no part of me tying her up.'

He would not be thwarted.

'I take the leotard that is around her neck already and I put my hands on it and pull it tight. She tries to stop me, but she can't and I keep pulling it tighter and tighter until she go.

'Then I get the nylons and put them around… I do not know for sure… it was a kind of haze… that I put two stockings… yes, two stockings went around her neck…

'I leave her on the bed and one of her legs is out and touching the floor… I recall the torn-away, pinkish-white blouse back off her shoulders and that she didn't have much else on.'

Twenty-three-year-old Joanne Graff had only moved to Lawrence four months earlier.

Change of heart?

Another year had passed and the Boston Strangler was still at large. He struck again on 4 January 1964. But somehow, with the murder of 19-year-old Mary Anne Sullivan – the youngest victim yet – DeSalvo felt that something had changed.

'She opened the door. She is wearing blue jeans, short ones, cut rough and uneven, and a yellow blouse. She let me in easy with the "work on your apartment" con.

'Once I get in, I say, "Where is everybody, anyway?"'

'She says, "Why, there's nobody here but me, who did you expect to be here?"'

'I say, "Well, you got roommates, haven't you?"'

'"Yes," she says, "but they are working today."'

He made the usual business of looking around the place.

'All the time I am building this thing up in wondering what kind of a body she had got and what she will look like… and I have to look at her to believe that a woman can be so trusting…'

In the kitchen, he showed her the knife with a blade about 5–6 in (13–15 cm) long.

'What is that for?' she asked.

'That is to keep you quiet,' I said.

'But what for?' she asked.

'I am going to take you into the bedroom,' he said. 'And I am going to make love to you.'

They went into the bedroom and he said, 'I am going to strip you and tie you up.'

'Why do you have to do that?' she asked. 'What is the matter with you, anyway?'

'She is one of the few women I have who asked me questions like that… only one other one asked me those kind of questions and that was Patricia Bissette, who was really good to me… when I think of what I did to her…'

'Just get on the bed,' he said.

'Let me go back now and tell you something I don't tell you before. She was working in the kitchen when I came to the door with a knife in her hand – it is a knife like you use for peeling vegetables. She was making supper for her roommates.

'In the bedroom, she said that she don't need to be tied… I take that to mean that she will do what I want without my forcing her, but I am now in a kind of haze and I say to her, "Keep quiet, don't scream, I am going to tie you… there is nothing you can do about it…"

'You know, all this time she still have this little knife in her hand, but I think that both of us forget that she has it. She is not trying to fight me, she is trying to talk to me, but what she don't know is that I can't really hear her…

'I begin to tie her with this thing I find there… a scarf of some kind… I used that to tie her hands. I tied her feet also… I tied them to the bottom of the bed. Yes, I had ripped her clothing off, most of it, there is only this part of a bra and part of her blouse over her breasts. I know that I hit her. Why did I do that?… she came at me and it was necessary to keep her quiet.'

That would not be the end of it.

Pointless pleading

'At the time, she was trying to talk me out of it and she say the wrong thing about my not being a very good man, being dirty… I hit her and once I start, I keep on. I hit her on the face, on the breasts and on the belly… she is not knocked out because she keeps talking.

'"Why don't you listen to me?" she says. "I am trying to reason with you… you don't have to do that… please don't do that to me… I am not going to make it hard for you… please try to understand…"

'Now she got me mad, real angry, and I rip off her clothes. I put a sweater over her head, so that she wouldn't be able to scream. Also, I don't want her to see me, but I don't want not to let her talk. It seems wrong just to shut her up completely. She is not a bad girl, she really tried to make me understand how it was she felt…'

It made no difference.

'She says that it is hot under there and I say, well, it has got to be that way. She says that she can't breathe too well. I don't pay no attention to that. I got her hands tied in front of her with this scarf and she is practically naked.

'I spread her legs, and I had intercourse with her. I bite her all over, I chew on her... and when I am done with that, I reach up and I strangle her with my hands, pressing my thumbs against her throat. She was fighting by this time. I was sitting on her hands while she fought viciously for life...

'But listen... I had intercourse with her... she was still alive... she allowed me to do it to her, you understand me? But that don't make no difference, I strangled her... face to face... using my thumbs against her Adam's apple.'

And that was that.

'After she was dead... I know that she was dead because I took the sweater off her head and looked at her... her eyes was still open and she was looking like she was surprised and... even... disappointed with the way I had treated her... I took the little knife that she had in her hand all the time and cut the scarf off her hands.

'It is strange, even sad... she did not once lift that knife against me, even to defend her life... she was a good person and yet I did all these things to her.

'I take that scarf I tied her with and cut it up and I go into the bathroom and flush it down the toilet. I come back and lift her up, so that she is kind of sitting with her back against the headboard of the bed.'

Even though she was dead, he kept talking to her.

'"I don't know why this is," I said to her. "But I can't help doing it."'

Nor did the abuse stop.

'I get on her on the bed, straddling her. I sit there for a minute, looking at her breasts and her face. I feel myself ready for it again and I masturbate. I hold myself out, so that the semen strike her right in the face. Then I get off and she is sitting there with that stuff on her nose and mouth and chin.'

He showed some awareness of the terrible things he had done.

'I am not in control of myself… I know that something awful has been done, that the whole world of human beings are shocked and will be even more shocked that people everywhere are saying, my God, is this a man?… But it can't be helped, I am what I am…'

Still, he would have to leave his trademark, so they would know it was the work of the Boston Strangler.

'I put a stocking around her throat and knot it twice, good and tight, then I find this pink scarf and tie that around her throat, tight, too… then I put a loose pink and white thing around and tied it in a big bow…'

Then it got worse.

'It is hard to talk about what I did then. I think, looking back on it, that it had something to do with this being a killing that was a mark… something like the end of something, you understand me?

'I went into the kitchen. I don't know why I did this. I get a broom and I go back out into the bedroom. She was on the bed. I stood there with the broom and looking at her I begin to get angry… she makes me angry, just to look at her, I don't know why…

'I go over to the bed and I take the broom handle and put it into her… I push it into her, but not so far as to hurt her. You say it is funny that I worry about hurting her when she is already dead, but that is the truth… I do not want to hurt her.

'I leave it there and she look like a woman with things being done to her. I stand there and look, then I go around the apartment again… I find this card, it says, "Happy New Year" – I go back to her and put it at her right foot. I lean it against her foot.'

It was all over.

End game

'When I go out of there, it was like it never happened. I mean it is just as if I was coming out of something. I got out and I got downstairs and you could of said you saw me upstairs and as far as I was concerned, it wasn't me. I can't explain it to you any other way. Lately, everything had been getting... strange... It's just so unreal. I was there. It was done. I don't deny it. And yet if you talked to me an hour later, a half-hour later, it didn't mean nothing, it just didn't mean nothing.

'This is the hardest one for me because I am realizing that these things are true, and that these things I did do, that I have read in books about, that other people do, that I didn't think or realize that I would ever do these things, that they are true and that I did them... the same things that I read about in detective books.

'I go down and out of that place and when I get to Charles Street it is dark... I even stand for a minute in the doorway and already the whole thing is fading out in my mind, but I want to tell you, that somehow I feel that something important has happened to me here... I don't know what... but I feel it. For just a minute, I stand there and it seems to me that no more women will ever see the Boston Strangler again.'

Although the Boston Strangler did not kill again, on 27 October 1964 a man broke into the apartment of a young newly-wed, tied her up and sexually assaulted her. Then, he apologized and left. When she described him to a police artist, detectives recognized him as the Measuring Man. Victims of similar rapes from all over New England identified him as their assailant and he was arrested.

But apart from his confession, there was no evidence that DeSalvo was the Boston Strangler. He was sentenced to life imprisonment for other offences and was stabbed to death in jail.

CHAPTER NINE

H. H. Holmes

Over 28 million visitors flocked to the World's Fair in Chicago in 1893. Some stayed at the World's Fair Hotel. They checked in, but rarely checked out. The hotel was essentially a three-storey murder factory. It was a maze of soundproofed corridors and rooms, torture chambers, gas chambers and dissection rooms, with false doors and chutes to deliver victims' remains to the basement for disposal in vats of acid and quick lime, or to be burnt in a crematorium. It became known as 'Murder Castle' when it was discovered that the owner, America's first serial killer, H. H. Holmes, had been murdering guests and selling their skeletons and other body parts. He admitted to killing 27, though the true body count may have been higher than 200.

Bodysnatcher, murderer, bigamist

Born Herman Webster Mudgett in New Hampshire in 1861, Holmes began his life of crime as a medical student, using corpses from the dissection lab where he worked to defraud life insurance companies. He was also suspected when a small boy disappeared. Holmes left town soon after.

He was working in a drugstore in Philadelphia when another boy died from medicine bought there. Again, he denied everything and quickly left the city. By then, he had changed his name to Henry

Howard Holmes to avoid detection for other scams. Along the way, he became a bigamist twice over.

Arriving in Chicago in 1886, he bought an empty lot where he began building his Murder Castle, defrauding investors and suppliers. His first-known victim was his mistress, Julia Smythe. Two more women he was involved with disappeared soon after. These were one-time actress, Minnie Williams, who he had taken on as a stenographer, and her sister, Annie. They vanished during a scheme he devised to defraud them.

Never a dull moment

Holmes also made money stealing the jewellery of his victims, harvesting their organs and selling their skeletons to medical schools. As guests at the hotel were largely visitors to the city, it was not known how many disappeared into Holmes' basement or simply went home or even perhaps moved on.

Holmes was arrested for selling mortgaged goods but was bailed out by a fellow criminal. Together, they planned to swindle an insurance company by taking out a life policy on Holmes and faking his death. That failed, but Holmes succeeded with a similar scheme by the simple expedient of murdering his business partner of eight years, Benjamin Pitezel, after taking out insurance on him. Holmes then took Pitezel's wife as his mistress and murdered two of her daughters by locking them in a trunk and pumping gas into it. Their naked bodies were later found in the cellar of a house he had rented in Toronto. Pitezel's son was then drugged, murdered, dismembered and burnt. His remains were found up the chimney in the house in Indianapolis that they were staying at in 1894. Holmes also made a failed attempt on the lives of Mrs Pitezel, another daughter named Dessie and her baby in Detroit.

Holmes was eventually arrested for horse theft in Texas in 1894. After the two girls' bodies were found in Toronto, the Chicago police began investigating the 'Castle'.

Herman Webster Mudgett, better known as H. H. Holmes.

In October 1895, Holmes was put on trial for the murder of Benjamin Pitezel, found guilty and sentenced to death. It was clear that Holmes had also murdered the Pitezel children. After initially confessing to 27 murders, he later increased the number to 130. Even this was thought to be an underestimate. He was hanged on 7 May 1896 after selling his story to the newspapers. Different versions of his confession appeared in *The Philadelphia Inquirer* and the *New York Journal*, which was republished in various regional papers, including *The Chicago Daily Inter-Ocean*.

Very image of the Devil

The day before the *Inquirer* ran Holmes' tale, *The Philadelphia North American* published excerpts based on their own look at advance copies of the handwritten original. But the portions they printed, including the famous Holmes quote: 'I was born with the Devil in me' section, didn't appear in the published confessions.

Another paragraph that does not appear in his confessions has survived: 'I am convinced that since my imprisonment I have changed woefully and gruesomely from what I was formerly in feature and figure. My features are assuming a pronounced satanical cast. I have become afflicted with that dread disease, rare but terrible, with which physicians are acquainted, but over which they have no control whatsoever. That disease is a malformation or distortion of the osseous parts... My head and face are gradually assuming an elongated shape. I believe fully that I am growing to resemble the devil – that the similitude is almost completed.'

These symptoms were not present when he was committing his crimes, but only started after his arrest.

'The first taking of human life that is attributed to me is the case of Dr Robert Leacock of New Baltimore, Michigan, a friend and former schoolmate. I knew that his life was insured for a large sum and, after enticing him to Chicago, I killed him by giving him an overwhelming dose of laudanum. My subsequently taking his dead body from place to place in and about Grand Rapids, Michigan, as has been an often-printed heretofore, and the risk and excitement attendant upon the collection of the 40,000 dollars of insurance were very insignificant matters compared with the torturing thought that I had taken human life.'

Holmes said that this occurred in 1886, though Leacock died on 5 October 1889 in Canada.

'For prior to this death... I begged to be believed in stating that I had never sinned so heavily either by thought or deed. Later, like the man-eating tiger of the tropical jungle, whose appetite for blood has once been aroused, I roamed about the world seeking whom I could destroy. Think of the awful list that follows. Twenty-seven lives, men and women, young girls and innocent children, plotted out by one monster's hand, and you, my reader of a tender and delicate nature, will do well to read no further, for I will in no way spare myself...'

Nor did he spare his victims.

The bodies pile up

'My second victim was Dr Russell, a tenant in the Chicago building recently renamed "The Castle". During a controversy concerning the nonpayment of rent due me, I struck him to the floor with a heavy chair, when he with one cry for help, ending in a groan of anguish, ceased to breathe.'

This seems to have been a Dr Russler who had an office in the Castle and disappeared in 1892.

Holmes thought of selling the body to a Chicago medical college. Instead, he sold it, and later others, to a man he would not name, who paid $25 to $45 a corpse.

'The third death was to a certain extent due to a criminal operation. A man and woman are cognizant of and partially responsible for both the operation and death. The victim was Mrs Julia L Conner.

A reference to almost any newspaper of August, 1895 will give the minute details of the horrors of this case, as they were worked out by the detectives, therefore, making it unnecessary to repeat it here, save to add that the death of the child Pearl, her little daughter, who is the fourth victim, was caused by poison, and that the man and woman above referred to for its administration, although it was at my instigation that it was done, as I believed the child was old enough to remember of her mother's sickness and death.'

Mrs Conner was Holmes' mistress. She and five-year-old Pearl disappeared on Christmas Eve 1891. Mrs Conner seems to have died when Holmes botched an abortion.

'The fifth murder, that of Rodgers, of West Morgantown, Virginia, occurred in 1888, at which time I was boarding there for a few weeks. Learning that the man had some money, I induced him to go upon a fishing trip with me, and being successful in allaying his suspicions, I finally ended his life by a sudden blow upon the head with an oar. The body was found about a month thereafter, but I was not suspected until after my trial...'

The local paper in Morgantown said that no man of that name had been murdered there, nor had there been a murder where the culprit had not been convicted. A man who looked like Holmes had been seen in the town, but it was not him.

Brutal assault

'The sixth case is that of Charles Cole, a Southern speculator. After considerable correspondence, this man came to Chicago, and I enticed him into the Castle, where, while I was engaging him in conversation, a confederate struck him a most vicious blow upon the head with a piece of gas pipe. So heavy was the blow, it not only caused his death without a groan and hardly a movement, but it crushed his skull to such an extent that his body was almost useless to the party who bought the body.'

A Milford Cole of Baltimore, Maryland disappeared after receiving a telegram from Holmes telling him to come to Chicago in July 1894.

'A domestic, named Lizzie, was the seventh victim. She, for a time, worked in the Castle restaurant and I soon learned that Quinlan was paying her too close attention and fearing lest it should progress so far that it would necessitate his leaving my employ I thought it wise to end the life of the girl. This I did by calling her to my office and suffocating her in the vault of which so much has since been printed, she being the first victim that died therein. Before her death, I compelled her to write letters to her relations and to Quinlan, stating that she had left Chicago for a Western State and should not return.'

Patrick Quinlan was a caretaker at the Castle. The vault was airtight. Victims lured in there were gassed or left to suffocate or starve to death.

Lambs to the slaughter

'The eighth, ninth and tenth cases are Mrs Sarah Cook, her unborn child, and Miss Mary Haracamp, of Hamilton, Canada. In 1888, Mr Frank Cook became a tenant in the Castle. He was engaged to be married to a young lady living at some distance from Chicago, who later came there and was married to him in my presence, by the Rev Dr Taylor, of Englewood, Illinois.

'They kept house in the Castle, and for a time I boarded with them. Shortly afterward, Miss Mary Haracamp, of Hamilton, a niece of Mrs Sarah Cook, came to Chicago and entered my employ as a stenographer. But Mrs Cook and her niece had access to all the rooms by means of a master key and, one evening while I was busily engaged preparing my last victim for shipment, the door suddenly opened and they stood before me. It was a time for quick action, rather than for words of explanation upon my part, and before they had recovered from the horror of the sight, they were within the fatal vault, so lately tenanted by the dead body, and then, after writing a letter at my dictation to Mr Cook that they had tired of their life with him and had gone away, not expecting to return, their lives were sacrificed instead of giving them their liberty in exchange for their promise to at once – and forever – leave Chicago, which had been promised them in return for writing the letter. These were particularly sad deaths, both on account of the victims being exceptionally upright and virtuous women and because Mrs Sarah Cook, had she lived, would have soon become a mother.'

Inspector John E Fitzpatrick, lead investigator on the Holmes case, seems to have dismissed these two victims. No one seems to have reported Mrs Cook or Mary Haracamp missing.

'Soon after this, Miss Emeline Cigrand, of Dwight, Illinois was sent to me by a Chicago typewriter firm to fill the vacancy of stenographer. She had formerly been employed at Dwight where she had become acquainted with a man who visited her from time to time while she was in my employ. She was finally engaged to him and the day set for their wedding. This attachment was particularly obnoxious to me, both because Miss Cigrand had become almost indispensable in my office work, and because she had become my mistress as well as stenographer.

'I endeavoured upon several occasions to take the life of the young man and, failing in this, I finally resolved that I would kill her instead, and upon the day of their wedding, even after cards had been sent out announcing that it had occurred, she came to my office to bid me goodbye. While there, I asked her to step inside the vault for some papers for me. There, I detained her, telling her that if she would write her husband that at the last moment she had found that it would be impossible to live happily with him and consequently had left Chicago in such a way that to search for her would be useless, I would take her to a distant city and live openly with her as my wife. She was very willing to do this and prepared to leave the vault upon completing the letter, only to learn that the door would never be again opened until she had ceased to suffer the tortures of a slow and lingering death.'

Emeline Cigrand was 21 at the time of her death in December 1892. Her skeleton was found in the home of a Chicago physician. Some of what was thought to be her hair was found in the Castle's cellar.

Three attempted murders

'Then follows an unsuccessful attempt to commit a triple murder for the $90 that my agent for disposing of "stiffs" would have given me for the bodies of the intended victims, who were three young women working in my restaurant upon Milwaukee Avenue, Chicago.

'That these women lived to tell their experience to the police last summer is due to my foolishly trying to chloroform all of them at one and the same time. By their combined strength, they overpowered me, and ran screaming into the street, clad only in their night robes. I was arrested next day, but was not prosecuted.

'To this attempt to kill could very justly be added my attempt to take the lives of Mrs Pitezel and two of her children at a later date, thus making the total number of my victims 33, instead of 27, as it was through no fault of mine that they escaped.'

Mrs Pitezel thought that Holmes had tried to kill her using nitroglycerin. A pit of quicklime was found in the basement, presumably prepared for the disposal of the bodies.

'My next attempt was carried out with more caution. The victim was a very beautiful young woman named Rosine Van Jassand, whom I induced to come into my fruit and confectionery store, and, once within my power, I compelled her to live with me there for a time, threatening her with death if she appeared before any of my customers. A little later, I killed her by administering ferro-cyanide of potassium. The location of this store was such that it would have been hazardous to have sent out a large box containing a body, and I therefore buried her remains in the store basement, and from day to day during the recent investigation at the Castle I expected to hear that excavations had been made there as well.'

The name Rosine Van Jassand appeared in the *Inquirer*, while the victim was named as Anna Van Tassaud in the *Journal*. This was thought to refer to Emily Van Tassel, who worked at Holmes' store on Milwaukee Avenue. She disappeared in June 1892. Later excavation of the basement of Holmes' store found nothing.

Death of an extortionist

'Robert Latimer, a man who had for some years been in my employ as janitor, was my next victim. Several years previous, before I had ever taken human life, he had known of certain insurance work I had engaged in, and when, in after years, he sought to extort money from me, his own death and the sale of his body was the recompense meted out to him.

'I confined him within the secret room and slowly starved him to death. Of this room and its secret gas supply and muffled windows and doors, sufficient has already been printed. Finally, needing its use for another purpose and because his pleadings had become almost unbearable, I ended his life. The partial excavation in the walls of this room found by the police was caused by Latimer's endeavouring to escape by tearing away the solid brick and mortar with his unaided fingers.'

Inspector Fitzpatrick announced that Robert Latimer was still alive. However *The Inter-Ocean* said that the man he had found was the wrong Robert Latimer.

'The 14th case is that of Miss Anna Betts, and was caused by my purposely substituting a poisonous drug in a prescription that had been sent to my drugstore to be compounded, believing that it was known that I was a physician, I should be called in to witness her death, as she lived very near the store. This was not the case, however, as the regular physician was in attendance at the time. The prescription, still on file at the Castle drugstore, should be considered by the authorities if they still are inclined to attribute this death to causes that reflect upon Miss Betts' moral character.'

In 1892, Virginia Anna Betts, a 24-year-old Canadian, died in her home a block away from the Castle. On her death certificate, the cause of death was given as 'apoplexy'. She was also suffering from 'heart disease', which lasted four days. Those symptoms could be attributed to poisoning. Elsewhere, Holmes denied murdering her, saying that he had been charged with killing her during a 'criminal operation' – that is, an abortion.

'The death of Miss Gertrude Conner, of Muscatine, Iowa, though not the next in order of occurrence, is so similar to the last that a description of one suffices for both, save in this case Miss Conner left Chicago immediately but did not die until she had reached her home in Muscatine. Perhaps these two cases show more plainly than any others the light regard I had for the lives of my fellow beings.'

Gertrude Conner appears to have been the sister-in-law of victim, Julia Conner. There are, again, stories that Holmes wanted her to run away with him but grew jealous when she fell for another man.

Lured to her doom

'The 16th murder is that of Miss Kate—, of Omaha, a young woman owning much valuable real estate in Chicago, where I acted as her agent. This was at the time so graphically described by a local writer as when I was allowed to hold property under one name, act as notary public under another and carried on a general business under still another title.

'I caused Miss Kate— to believe that a favourable opportunity had come for her to convert her holdings into cash, and having accomplished this for her, she came to Chicago and I paid her the money, taking a receipt in full for same, and thus protected myself in the event of an inquiry at a later date.

'I asked her to look about my offices and finally to look within the vault, and, having once passed that fatal door, she never came forth alive. She did not die at once, however, and her anger when first she realized that she was deprived of her liberty, then her offer of the entire 40,000 dollars in exchange for same and finally her prayers are something terrible to remember. It was stated that I had also killed a sister of Miss Kate— but I think this report has already been contradicted.'

This was Kate Durkee of Omaha, who did have dealings with Holmes. However, she issued a statement saying that she was very much still alive.

Vaporized

'The next death was that of a man named Warner, the originator of the Warner Glass Bending Company, and here again a very large sum of money was realized, which prior to his death had been deposited in two Chicago banks, nearly all of which I secured by means of two checks, made out and properly signed by him for a small sum each. To these I later added the word "thousand", and the necessary numbers, and by passing them through the bank where I had a regular open account…

'It will now be remembered that the remains of a large kiln made of fire brick was found in the Castle basement. It had been built under Mr Warner's supervision for the purpose of exhibiting his patents. It was so arranged that in less than a minute after turning on a jet of crude oil atomized with steam the entire kiln would be filled with a colourless flame, so intensely hot iron would be melted therein.

'It was into this kiln that I induced Mr Warner to go with me, under pretence of wishing certain minute explanations of the process, and then stepping outside, as he believed to get some tools, I closed the door and turned on the oil and steam to their full extent. In a short time, not even the bones of my victim remained. The coat found outside the kiln was the one he took off before going therein.'

Although Warner had been a business associate of Holmes, there is no evidence that the latter murdered him.

'In 1891, I associated myself in business with a young Englishman, whose name I am more than willing to publish to the world, but I am advised it could not be published on my unsupported statement, who by his own admission, had been guilty of all other forms of wrongdoing, save murder, and presumably of that as well. To manipulate certain real estate securities we held, so as to have them secure us a good commercial rating was an easy matter for him and he was equally able to interest certain English capitalists in patents, so that for a time it seemed that in the near future our greatest concern would be how to dispose of the money that seemed about to be showered upon us. By an unforeseen occurrence, our rating was destroyed and it became necessary to at once raise a large sum and this was done by my partner enticing to Chicago a wealthy banker named Rogers from a (north) Wisconsin town in such a manner that he could have left no intelligence with whom his business was to be.

'To cause him to go in the Castle and within the secret room under the pretence that our patents were there was easily brought about, more so than to force him to sign checks and drafts for 70,000 dollars, which we had prepared. At first, he refused to do so, stating that his liberty, that we offered him in exchange, would be useless to him without his money, that he was too old to again hope to make another fortune. Finally, by alternately starving him and nauseating him with the gas, he was made to sign the securities, all of which were converted into money and by my partner's skill as a forger in such a manner as to leave no trace of their having passed through our hands.

'I waited with much curiosity to see what propositions my partner would advance for the disposal of our prisoner, as I well knew he, no more than I, contemplated giving him his liberty. My partner evidently waited with equal expectancy for me to suggest what should be done, and I finally made preparation to allow him to leave the building, thus forcing him to suggest that he be killed. I would only consent to this upon the condition that he should administer the chloroform, and leave me to dispose of the body as my part of the work... That evening, this large sum of money was equally divided between us...'

Inspector Fitzpatrick said that Rodgers was pure fiction. While searching the Castle, amateur detective, Robert Corbitt, said he found letters to Holmes from an Englishman named William Green, who lived in Chicago for a while and may have been the mysterious Englishman who Holmes blamed for Rodgers' murder.

Coffin-shaped box

'The 19th case is that of a woman, whose name has passed from my memory, who came to the Castle restaurant to board. A tenant of

HOLMES' "CASTLE"   (*63d St*, *Chicago, Ill.*)

H. H. Holmes's murder castle in Chicago.

mine at the time immediately became very much infatuated with the woman, who he learned was a widow and wealthy. This tenant was married, and his wife occasionally came to the restaurant when this boarder was there, which did not tend to decrease a family quarrel that for quite a time had threatened this tenant's family with disruption. Finally, he came to me for advice, and I was very willing to have him in my power in order that I could later use him in my work if need be. I suggested that he live with the woman in the Castle for a time, and later if his life became unpleasant to him, we would kill her and divide her wealth.

'Soon, he suggested it was time to take his companion's life. This was done by my administering chloroform while he controlled her violent struggles. It was the body of this woman within the long coffin-shaped box that was taken from the Castle late in 1893, of which the police were notified.'

There is no evidence to confirm this, but there has been speculation that the mysterious tenant was Johann Hoch, who was in Chicago at the time. A serial bigamist, Hoch married wealthy widows or divorcees and had proposed to what was thought to have been his 55th wife when he was arrested in 1905. He would swindle them out of all their money and either leave them or poison them with arsenic. The police were certain that he had killed 15 – it may have been as many as 50. But he went to the gallows for a single homicide.

A virtuous woman seduced

'The Williams sisters come next. In order that these deaths may be more fully understood, it is necessary for me to state that what has been said by Miss Minnie R Williams' Southern relatives regarding her pure and Christian life should be believed; alas, that prior to her meeting me in 1893, she was a virtuous woman…'

He then retracted numerous scurrilous allegations he had made about her.

'I first met Miss Minnie R Williams in New York in 1888, where she knew me as Edward Hatch, and later under the same name in Denver, as has been testified by certain young women who recognized my photograph. Early in 1893, I was again introduced to her as H. H. Holmes in the office of Campbell & Dowd, of Chicago, to whom she had applied for them to secure her a position as a stenographer. Soon after entering my employ, I induced her to give me $2,500 in money and to transfer to me by deed $50,000 worth of Southern real estate and, a little later, to live with me as my wife, all this being easily accomplished owing to her innocent and childlike nature, she hardly knowing right from wrong in such matters.

'Thereafter, I succeeded in securing two checks from her for $2,500 and $1,000 each, and I also learned that she had a sister, Nannie, in Texas who was an heir to some property and induced Miss Minnie Williams to have her come to Chicago upon a visit. Upon her arrival, I met her at the depot and took her to the Castle, telling her Miss Minnie Williams was there. It was an easy matter to force her to assign to me all she possessed. After that, she was immediately killed in order that no one in or about the Castle should know of her having been there, save the man who burned her clothing. It was the footprint of Nannie Williams, as later demonstrated by that most astute lawyer and detective, Mr Copps, of Fort Worth, that was found upon the painted surface of the vault door made during her violent struggles before her death.

'It was also easy to give to Miss Minnie Williams a delayed letter, stating that her sister's proposed visit had been given up and also, by intercepting later letters and substituting others, to keep her from learning that the sister had left the South. Having secured all the money and property Miss Williams had, it was time that she were killed.

'Owing to a fire that had occurred in the Castle, I was unable to resort to the usual methods in taking her life, and after some delay, took her to Momence, Illinois about November 15, 1893, registering at a hotel near the post-office under an assumed name, but as man and wife. My intention was to quietly kill her in some sure manner, but a freight wreck that occurred upon the outskirts of the town the day following my arrival there, which, out of curiosity, I visited, brought me in contact with a passenger conductor named Peck, who knew me, and I therefore abandoned it, but later returned and took her eight miles East of Momence upon a freight line that is little used, and ended her life with poison and buried her body in the basement of the house spoken of at about the time of the Irvington discovery in 1895.

'It was a great wonder that the body was not found at the time if the detectives in reality went to that location. Nothing would at the present time give me so much satisfaction as to know that her body had been properly buried, and I would be willing to give up the few remaining days I have to live, if by so doing this could be accomplished, for, because of her spotless life before she knew me, because of the large amount of money I defrauded her of, because I killed her sister and brother, because not being satisfied with all this, I endeavoured after my arrest to blacken her good name by charging her with the death of her sister, and later with the instigation of the murder of the three Pitezel children, endeavouring to have it believed that her motive for so doing was to afford an avenue of escape for herself if ever apprehended for her sister's death, by pointing to her as a wholesale murderess, and, therefore, presumably guilty of the sister's death as well; for all these reasons, this is without exception the saddest and most heinous of any of my crimes.'

The mysterious Edward Hatch

The 'Irvington discovery' was the discovery of the body of Howard Pitezel there. Indeed, Holmes had said before that Minnie Williams had killed her sister Anna, or 'Nannie', by hitting her over the head with an office stool in a fit of jealousy. When he was first arrested,

Holmes maintained that Minnie and the Pitezel children were alive and in England.

He later said that Minnie had taken up with the mysterious Edward Hatch, who, he said, he assumed had murdered the Pitezels. It was only in his published confessions that he admitted using the name Edward Hatch himself.

Minnie Williams came from Texas and went to work for Holmes in the Castle. They became romantically involved. Minnie then wrote to her sister, telling her to come to Chicago as she was to be married.

Holmes and Minnie were living together in an apartment on the North Side as Mr and Mrs Henry Gordon. Anna's trunk was sent there. While Minnie was visiting Milwaukee, Anna took over as house-keeper. They visited the World's Fair together. Meanwhile, Holmes was building what was thought to be a new Castle on land in Fort Worth that Minnie owned.

On 4 July, Anna wrote to an aunt that she, Minnie and a mysterious 'Brother Harry' were heading for Europe. Minnie and Anna were last seen alive together the next day. Two days after that, Holmes quit the apartment. According to the version of the story he told after he had been arrested, he had been out of town, returning to find Minnie screaming, 'I thought you would never return. Nannie is dead.' His story was that they had been fighting over him, with Minnie accusing Anna of stealing her husband. Minnie had then killed Anna and Holmes had dumped her body in the lake.

The project in Fort Worth did not come off as the banks suspected that Holmes was forging Minnie's signature on the documents deeding the property to him. He then married Georgiana Yoke bigamously in Denver.

Buried in sandy soil

'A man who came to Chicago to attend the Chicago Exposition, but whose name I cannot recall, was my next victim. The Chicago authorities can, if they choose, learn the name by inquiries made of the Hartford Insurance Company…

'I determined to use this man in my various business dealings, and did so for a time, until I found he had not the ability I had first thought he possessed, and I therefore decided to kill him. This was done, but as I had not had any dealings with the "stiff dealer" for some time previous to this murder, I decided to bury the body in the basement of the house that I formerly owned near the corner of Seventy-fourth and Honore streets, in Chicago, where, by digging deeply in the sandy soil, the body will be found.

'After Miss Williams' death, I found among her papers an insurance policy made in her favour by her brother, Baldwin Williams, of Leadville, Col. I therefore went to that city early in 1894, and, having found him, took his life by shooting him, it being believed I had done so in self-defence. A little later, when the assignment of the policy to which I had forged Miss Williams' name was presented to John M Maxwell, of Leadville, the administrator of the Williams estate, it was honoured and the money paid. Both in this instance and that of a $1,000 check given to Dr Tolman and checks aggregating $2,500 by I R Hitt & Co, both of Chicago, inasmuch as the endorsements are forgeries, the Williams heirs can now recover these amounts, although it will be an undeserved hardship upon those who have once advanced the money upon them.'

No one identified this man and no body was found, so it is impossible to know whether Holmes was telling the truth.

Grisly end

'Benjamin F Pitezel comes next… It will be understood that, from the first hour of our acquaintance, even before I knew he had a family who would later afford me additional victims for the gratification of my bloodthirstiness, I intended to kill him…

'Pitezel left his home for the last time late in July, 1894, a happy, light-hearted man, to whom trouble or discouragements of any kind were almost unknown. We then journeyed together to New York and later to Philadelphia, where the fatal house upon Callowhill Street in which he met his death September 2, 1894, was hired. Then came my writing to him the discouraging letters, purporting to be from his wife, causing him to again resort to drink....

'After thus preparing, I went to the house, quietly unlocked the door and stole noiselessly within and to the second-story room, where I found him insensibly drunk, as I had expected...

'Only one difficulty presented itself. It was necessary for me to kill him in such a manner that no struggle or movement of his body should occur, otherwise his clothing being in any way displaced it would have been impossible to again put them in a normal condition. I overcame this difficulty by first binding him hand and foot, and having done that, I proceeded to burn him alive by saturating his clothing and his face with benzine and igniting it with a match.

'So horrible was this torture that, in writing of it, I have been tempted to attribute his death to some humane means – not with a wish to spare myself, but because I fear that it will not be believed that one could be so heartless and depraved... The least I can do is to spare my reader a recital of the victim's cries for mercy, his prayers and finally, his plea for a more speedy termination of his sufferings, all of which upon me had no effect.

'Finally, when he was dead, I removed the straps and ropes that had bound him and extinguished the flames, and a little later, poured into his stomach one and one half ounces of chloroform.

'It has been asked why I did this after I knew that he was dead, what possible use it could have served? My answer to this is that I placed it there, so that at the time of the post-mortem examination, which I knew would be held, the Coroner's physician would be warranted in reporting that the death was accidental... and upon receipt of such intelligence, I believed the insurance company would at once pay the full amount of the claim...

'After his death, I gathered together various assignments of patents and deeds to property he had held for me that I had been careful to have him sign some days before, so I should not suffer pecuniary loss... I left the house without the slightest feeling of remorse for my terrible acts.'

The murder of Benjamin Pitezel is the only one that Holmes was brought to trial for. His confession is all the more remarkable since his attorneys were trying to appeal the verdict at the time and, after its publication, Holmes surprisingly went back to his original story that Pitezel had committed suicide.

'For one month and six days thereafter I took no human life, although about three weeks after Pitezel's death, I was afforded an opportunity to gratify my feverish lust for blood by going to the graveyard where he had been buried and under pretence of securing certain portions of his body for microscopical examination removed the same with a knife, and the heartless manner in which I did this and the evident gratification it afforded me has been most forcibly told by Mr Smith upon the witness stand...'

At Holmes' trial, his attorneys called no witnesses and presented no evidence. They argued that the prosecution had not proved their case beyond a reasonable doubt. The jury found otherwise.

Here, Holmes makes the point that he had gone for one month and six days without killing as if this was remarkable. Confessing to 27 murders – the first in 1886, the last in 1894 – would mean, on average, one every three-and-a-half months. This implies that there were many more murders.

Insurance scam

'The Irvington, Indiana, tragedy is next. Upon the 1st day of October, 1894, I took the three Pitezel children to the Circle House in Indianapolis, where I engaged permanent board for them until such a time as I could kill one or more of them. Upon the evening of that day,

I went to St Louis, where I remained until October 4, busily engaged in settling up the insurance matter with McDonalds and Howe, the attorneys. During this time, I also called upon the agent or owner of the Irvington house…

'On October 7th, I called at the Irvington drugstore and purchased the drugs I needed to kill the boy and, the following evening, I again went to the same store and bought an additional supply, as I feared I had not obtained a sufficient quantity upon my first visit…

'Early in the afternoon of October 10th, I had the boy's trunk and a stove I had bought taken to the depot, and they arrived at the Irvington house at about 6pm at which time Mr Moreman was the last person who saw the boy alive, for almost immediately I called him into the house and insisted that he go to bed at once, first giving him the fatal dose of medicine.

'As soon as he had ceased to breathe, I cut his body into pieces that would pass through the door of the stove and, by the combined use of gas and corncobs, proceeded to burn it with as little feeling as though it had been some inanimate object. If I could now recall one circumstance, a dollar of money to be gained, a disagreeable act or word upon his part, in justification of this horrid crime, it would be a satisfaction to me; but to think that I committed this and other crimes for the pleasure of killing my fellow beings, to hear their cries for mercy and pleas to be allowed even sufficient time to pray and prepare for death – all this is now too horrible for even me, hardened criminal that I am, to again live over without a shudder.

'Is it to be wondered at that since my arrest my days have been those of self-reproaching torture, and my nights of sleepless fear? Or that even before my death, I have commenced to assume the form and features of the Evil One himself?'

The murder took place while Holmes was somehow escorting three parties across the US and Canada. One group was seven-year-old, Howard, nine-year-old, Nellie, and 13-year-old, Alice, who Mrs

Pitezel had assigned to his care. There was Mrs Pitezel, her baby and her daughter, Dessie. Then there was Holmes' new wife, Georgiana Yoke.

Heartless fiend

'I now, with much reluctance, come to the discussion of the 26th and 27th murders. The victims were Alice and Nellie Pitezel, whose deaths will seem to many to be the saddest of all, both on account of the terribly heartless manner in which it was accomplished, and because in one instance, that of Alice, the oldest of these children, her death was the least of the wrongs suffered at my hands... the mental condition of the child upon the following day, would, if called for, be sufficient to decide the matter.

'These children, after boarding in Detroit for about one week, reached Toronto, October 19, and were taken to the Albion Hotel, where they boarded until they were killed. Upon October 20, I hired the Vincent Street house, having the lease made in the name of H M Howard, in order to avert suspicion as much as possible in case an investigation followed.

'Between 5 and 6pm the same day, I took a large empty trunk to the house... upon the 25th, the fatal day of these deaths, they were seen at the house at 1pm, and a little later they accompanied me to several clothing stores.

'Finally, at 4pm, while they were in a restaurant nearby, I entered a large store in which I believed I should meet Mrs Pitezel, holding in my hands some heavy winter underwear I had bought for the little boy already dead. Of this meeting, Mrs Pitezel has said, "I believe my children were at that time in that store with me."

'I immediately took them to the Vincent Street house and compelled them to get within the large trunk, through the cover of which I made a small opening. Here, I left them until I could return and at my leisure kill them. At 5pm, I borrowed a spade of a neighbour and at the same time called on Mrs Pitezel at her hotel. I then returned to my hotel and ate my dinner, and at 7pm went again to Mrs Pitezel's hotel, and aided her in leaving Toronto for Ogdensburg, NY. Later than 8pm, I again returned to the house where the children were imprisoned, and ended their lives by connecting the gas pipes with the trunk.

'Then came the opening of the trunk and the viewing of their little blackened and distorted faces, then the digging of their shallow graves in the basement of the house, the ruthless stripping off of their clothing and the burial without a particle of covering save the cold earth, which I heaped upon them with fiendish delight.

'Consider what an awful act this was! These little innocent and helpless children, the oldest only being 13 years of age, a puny and sickly child, who to look at one would believe much younger; consider that for eight years before their death I had been almost as much a father as though they had been my own children...'

Holmes said of Alice that death was the least of the wrongs suffered at his hands. In Philadelphia, she had been forced to identify the rotting corpse of her father. That night, it was alleged, Holmes raped her.

'From Toronto I went to Ogdensburg, from there to Burlington, Vermont, where I hired a furnished house for Mrs Pitezel's use, and a few days prior to my arrest in Boston I wrote her a letter in which I directed her to carry a bottle of dynamite that I had previously left in the basement, so arranged that in taking it to the third story of the house it would fall from her hands, and not only destroy her life, but that of her two remaining children, who I knew would be with her at the time. This was my last act, and happily it did not have a fatal termination.'

The confession was signed by H. H. Holmes. Less than four weeks after it was published, Holmes was hanged.

CHAPTER TEN

Carl Panzram

While in jail in Washington, DC in 1928, Carl Panzram wrote a 20,000-word confession. He began by listing the 17 prisons he had spent time in since 1903 when he was 12. And he was unrepentant.

'In my lifetime, I have murdered 21 human beings, I have committed thousands of burglaries, robberies, larcenies, arsons and, last but not least, I have committed sodomy on more than 1,000 male human beings,' he said. 'For all of these things, I am not the least bit sorry. I have no conscience, so that does not worry me. I don't believe in man, God nor Devil. I hate the whole damned human race, including myself.'

Mean-minded

Panzram was born on a small farm in Minnesota in 1891 to a family of 'honest and hard-working people. All except myself. I have been a human animal ever since I was born. When I was very young at five or six years of age, I was a thief and a liar, and a mean, despicable one at that. The older I got, the meaner I got.'

He was kicked around as a kid. 'It seemed to me then and still does now that everything was always right for the one who was the strongest and every single thing that I done was wrong. Everybody said so anyway.'

At the age of 11, he decided to leave home.

'Before I left, I looked around and figured that one of our neighbours who was rich and had a nice home full of nice things, he had too much and I had too little. So, one night I broke into his home and stole everything that to my eyes had the most value,' he said.

Carrying a pistol under his coat, he walked to the railroad yard where he jumped on a freight train going west, intending to become a cowboy and shoot Indians. But he was caught, 'beaten half to death' and sent to the Minnesota State Training School.

'Right there and then, I began to learn about man's inhumanity to man,' he said. 'They started me off by trying to beat the Christian religion into me and the consequences were that the more they beat and whipped me, the more I hated them and their damn religion.'

It gave him a thirst for retribution.

Life of punishment

'If I couldn't injure those who injured me, then I would injure someone else. From that day to this, I have followed that line of thought. From the time I was 12 years old, I have been in jail almost continuously until now when I am 36. I have spent 20 years of my life in prison. During my 20 years in all the various prisons and jails I have been in, I have undergone every kind of abuse and punishment that the ingenious minds of many men could devise and, believe me, men can surely figure out some horrible tortures to impose on other men. I have had the Whip, the Paddle, the Snorting Pole, the Humming Bird, the Hose and the Jacket. I have been chained up frontwards, backwards, bucked and gagged, spread-eagled, water-cured, starved, beaten, thrown into sweat boxes and half-cooked, thrown into ice-cold dungeons and half frozen. I have been in solitary confinement for years at a time where I could have no privileges or pleasures of any kind. Every single thing in life that men hold worthwhile and that go to make life worth living for, I have been denied and deprived of.'

The worst of the punishments was to be stripped naked, tied down with a towel soaked in salt water on the back, then beaten with a strap with holes in it that brought up little blisters that burst. This was the way he was taught to love Jesus.

'Naturally, I now love Jesus very much. Yes, I love him so damn much that I would like to crucify him all over again.'

Bent on revenge

To get his own back, he would urinate in the staff's coffee or masturbate in their dessert and watch them eat it. After a failed escape attempt, he was beaten black and blue. He responded by trying to put rat poison in the warden's rice pudding. The result was another beating, so he burnt the place down.

Feigning to be reformed, he was paroled after two years. As well as being taught by Christians to be a hypocrite, 'I had learned more about stealing, lying, hating, burning and killing. I had learned that a boy's penis could be used for something besides to urinate with and that a rectum would be used for other purposes than crepitating [sic].'

Once free, he was sent to a local German Lutheran Church school. But when the teacher began beating him, Panzram got a gun. His family beat him instead and he ran away again. This time, he reached the Pacific Coast, getting by through begging, telling lies and stealing. In a box car, he was raped by four burly hobos. It was to happen again.

'After I had hoboed around the country for a few months, I was finally caught in a small petty larceny burglary at Butte, Montana.'

After a stretch in the county jail, he was sent to another reform school. When one of the officers made life miserable for him, Panzram decided to kill him and hit him over the head with a thick oak board with a weight of iron on one end. He was still too young to go to state prison. 'So, they worked me hard and beat me harder. You see, they were trying to make a good boy of me. They took me in the hospital and operated on me by clipping my foreskin off to stop me from the habit of masturbation.'

He escaped with another boy.

Learning the ropes

'He showed me how to work the stick-up racket and how to rob the poor boxes in churches. I, in turn, taught him how to set fire to a church after we robbed it.'

Meanwhile, they sabotaged freight cars.

'By the time we got as far east as Fargo, North Dakota, we had between us, two good six-shooters, each had a good suit and about $150.00 in cash, besides various assortments of watches, rings and other slum that we had got by the burglary route and by harvesting the harvesters.'

They split up and Panzram joined the Army.

'I was only in the Army a month or two when I got three years in the US Military Prison at Fort Leavenworth, Kansas.'

He tried to escape, but when that failed he set fire to the prison. He was court-martialled and given three years' hard labour wearing a ball and chain. The case was reviewed by the then Secretary of War, William Howard Taft.

'Fourteen years later, I had the very good fortune to rob him out of about $40,000 worth of jewellery and liberty bonds.'

Ostensibly reformed, he was released. It was a sham.

'All that I had in my mind at that time was a strong determination to raise plenty of hell with anybody and everybody in every way I could and every time and every place I could,' he said. 'I was the spirit of meanness personified. I had not, at this time, got so that I hated myself; I only hated everybody else.'

Sacked at gunpoint from a mule-skinners' camp, he bought a gun in Denver, figuring to take over the red light district. Instead, he woke up in an alley with no gun, no money and no shoes, and a lump on his head. He also had gonorrhoea.

'I began to suspect that the ladies were very good things to leave alone.'

Ceaseless turmoil

Sacked from a Wild West show for fighting, he stole from the Kansas State Militia. When the Carnival Company turned up in Sedalia, Missouri, he burned down their tents. Then he took on a job as a strike-breaker. Along the way, he fought almost everyone he came into contact with.

The US Army was fighting in Mexico, so he headed south to rob churches there, but got arrested in Jacksonville, Texas and was sent

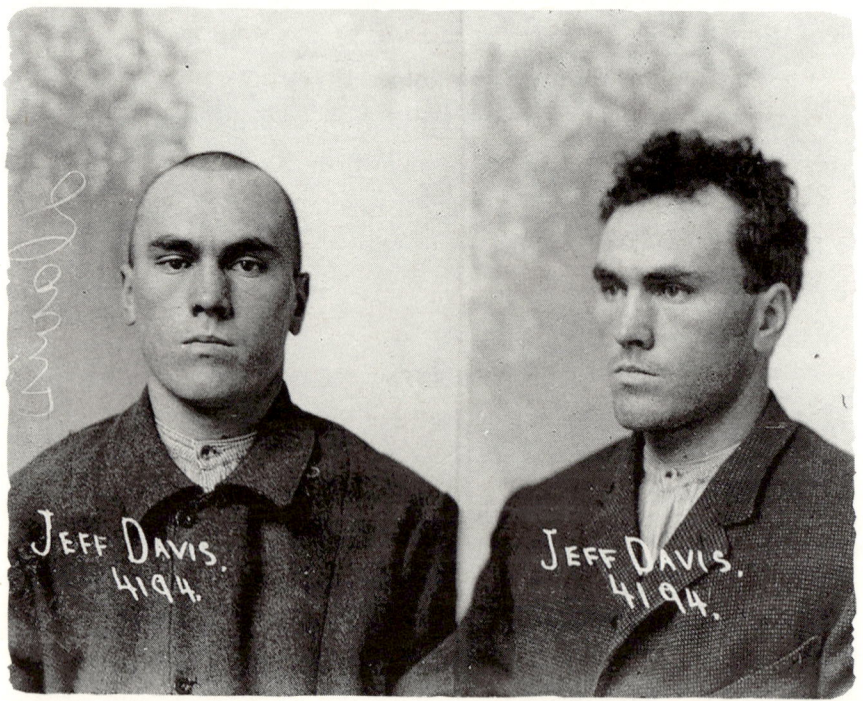

Carl Panzram, under one of his many aliases, 'Jefferson Davis', in mugshots taken at Montana State Prison in 1913.

to a country road gang, where the boss stole his catamite. He tried to escape more than once, even though he wore a ball and chain.

Eventually fleeing to Palestine, Texas, he found the town on fire, a sight he enjoyed.

'Several times people asked me to help them save their valuables. Sure, I helped 'em...'

Teaming up with an Indian, together they robbed a man and left him tied to a tree, but not before Panzram had sodomized him.

Crossing the border, he tried to join the Mexican Army, but was rejected. Instead, he joined the Foreign Legion, 'but all the churches I ever saw had all been robbed before I got there'. He stole his horse and everything that wasn't tied down and headed back to the US. There, he robbed chicken coops and barns, and set them on fire. Otherwise, he would set fire to woods and grasslands, or take pot shots at the windows of farmers' houses and cut loose the horses or cows he saw in the fields.

Riding freight trains, he would shoot at anything he fancied and robbed and sodomized hobos.

'I rode 'em old and young, tall and short, white and black. It made no difference to me at all, except that they were human beings.'

Bringer of chaos

He carried a Bible, so he could play the God-fearing man if arrested. It usually worked, but in Fresno he was sentence to 120 days for stealing a bicycle. He escaped after 30. Fleeing on a train, the brakeman tried to throw him off. When Panzram pulled a gun, he handed over his watch and chain, and all the cash he had.

'Then, he was so kind as to pull his pants down while I rode him around the floor of the freight car.'

Panzram then forced two other hobos to sodomize the brakeman at gunpoint.

In Dalles, Oregon, he was arrested for highway robbery, assault and sodomy, and jailed with a safe-blower named Cal Jordan, who was transferred to Moscow, Idaho before he had taught Panzram to blow safes. So, Panzram broke out, went to Moscow and tried to get Cal out – only to get caught and jailed himself.

'The thanks I got from old Cal was that he thought I was in love with him and he tried to mount me, but I wasn't broke to ride and he was, so I rode him.'

In jail again in Harrison, Idaho, he tried to break out again by setting fire to the jail and found himself in another jail. In Chinook, Montana, he pleaded guilty to burglary and got a year in state prison where he met up with an old friend from reform school. There, he swapped cellmates regularly.

'I knew more about sodomy than old boy Oscar Wilde ever thought of knowing,' he said. 'I was so busy committing sodomy that I didn't have any time left to serve Jesus as I had been taught to do in those reform schools.'

After two weeks' freedom, he was arrested for burglary again. Offered a light sentence for a guilty plea, he was duped and given seven years. Escaping from his cell, he smashed up the jail and set fire to it.

Behind bars again

In Oregon State Prison, another prisoner he encouraged to escape killed the warden. After several attempts to escape himself – and getting beaten for his pains – he stole some liquor and got the other prisoners drunk, hoping to escape in the confusion. When that did not work, he set fire to the jail. That earned him 61 days in the cooler.

When two other prisoners escaped, Panzram and an accomplice were stripped naked, chained to a door and hosed down with a fire hose, 'until we were black and blue, deaf and half-blind'. An investigation into maltreatment resulted in a softer regime. The new warden said that, if Panzram gave his word that he would not escape, he would open the prison gates and let him walk out. Surprising himself, Panzram did not abscond.

Instead, he became a trustee and joined the prison band and basketball team, who were allowed to play all over the state. But there was a hospital nearby and he began dating nurses. One of them supplied him with drink. One night, drunk, the temptation to decamp proved too much.

A week later, he broke into a house, ate his fill and stole a suit of clothes and a gun. The result was a gunfight with the local sheriff. He got two years for burglary and eight for shooting at the sheriff. Locked up, he broke out and escaped, evading a state-wide manhunt.

Registering under a false name, he held up a hotel in Frederick, Maryland. In New York, he signed on as a deckhand and sailed to Panama. He jumped ship and went to work in copper mines in Chile and Peru. Working as a foreman back in Panama, he was fired for fighting everyone. He planned to steal a schooner and kill the crew of six, but his accomplice got drunk, and so he did it single-handed.

Panzram sailed for Scotland on an oil tanker. Arriving in Glasgow, he robbed the ship and everyone on her, ending up in Barlinnie jail. From there, he went to London, Paris and Hamburg, before taking a ship back to the States.

More mayhem

Landing in Bridgeport, Connecticut, he robbed a jewellery store, then he sailed back to Hamburg where he spent $1,500 ($24,000/£19,000 today) in nine days – at 60 marks to the dollar. Broke, he returned to the US.

It was then, in New Haven, Connecticut, that he robbed the house of William Howard Taft who, in the meantime, had been president of the United States. He used the proceeds to buy a yacht.

He hired a crew, got them drunk, sodomized then killed them. He got more booze by robbing other yachts. The bodies were thrown overboard a mile from shore. He disposed of ten in three weeks.

Then he sailed for Atlantic City, but his yacht was wrecked on the way and all the stolen goods on board were lost. Heading back to Bridgeport, he served six months for burglary. Then he joined a seamen's strike and got involved in a shoot-out with scab sailors and the police. Arrested for aggravated assault and inciting a riot, he skipped bail and sailed to Europe, robbing the ship once he got there. Then, he went to Angola where he decided to have an African girl.

'I bought her from her mother and father for 80 escudos or about $8 in American money. The reason I paid such a big price for her was because she was a virgin,' he said. 'She was about 11 or 12 years old. I took her to my shack the first night and took her back to her father's shack the next. I demanded my money back because they had deceived me by saying the girl was a virgin. I didn't get my money back, but they gave me another and younger girl. This girl was about eight years old. I took her to my shack and maybe she was a virgin, but it didn't look like it to me. I took her back and quit looking for any more virgins.'

Instead, he took a boy and sodomized him.

'He told my boss and the boss-man fired me quickly, but before he did I licked the hell out of him.'

In Luanda, he found another boy who was 11 or 12. He took him to a gravel pit outside town and sodomized and killed him.

'His brains were coming out of his ears when I left him and he will never be any deader.'

Down the coast, he hired a canoe and six Africans and went to look for crocodiles. He killed all six. 'The crocs did the rest.'

No end to his troubles

Back in Luanda, he went to the house of a Spanish prostitute and robbed her of 10,000 escudos. With the police after him, he fled to the Belgian Congo. Then, he stowed away on an American ship. Marooned on the Gold Coast, he stole the money to get to the Canary Islands, where the American consul bought him a ticket for Lisbon.

He stowed away on the coal ship to England, then sailed to New York, where he began to look for another yacht to steal.

'In July at Salem, Massachusetts, I murdered an 11- or 12-year-old boy by beating his brains out with a rock. I tried a little sodomy on him first. I left him lying there with his brains coming out of his ears.'

Then he headed back towards New York – 'robbing and hell-raising as I came'.

Moving on to Louisiana, he checked into a hospital.

'When I left this hospital, I robbed their drug-room of two suitcases full of drugs, cocaine, morphine and opium. Sold some in New Orleans, some in St Louis and the rest in New York.'

In Yonkers, he took a job as a watchman.

'While there, I met a young boy 14 or 15 years old, whose name was George and whose home was and is in Yonkers. I started to teach him the fine art of sodomy, but I found that he had been taught all about it and he liked it fine.'

Seaborne menace

Then, Panzram became the watchman at the New Haven Yacht Club.

'I took very good care of their boats, so much so that I robbed one the next night. The name of the yacht I don't know, but the owner of it was the Police Commissioner of New Rochelle, NY, or some place near there.'

He stole another yacht in Providence, Rhode Island and sailed around picking up boys. In Kingston, New York, he changed the name of the yacht and tried to sell it, but he suspected the purchaser was trying to stick him up and shot him twice.

'After I killed him, I tied a big hunk of lead around him with a rope and threw him and his gun overboard. He is there yet, so far as I know. Then I sailed down the river stealing everything I could as I went.'

His boyfriend, George, got scared. When he returned home to Yonkers, the police were waiting. Panzram was arrested and charged with sodomy, burglary, robbery and trying to break out of jail. A lawyer got him out in exchange for the yacht, but when he tried to register it, the owner came to repossess her.

'A few days later, I went to New Haven where I killed another boy. I committed a little more sodomy on him also and then tied his belt around his neck and strangled him, picked him up when he was dead and threw his body over behind some bushes.'

In New York, he secured a berth on an Army transport ship bound for China. Before it sailed, he was discharged for being drunk and fighting. The next night, he robbed the express office at Larchmont, New York, but was caught in the act. Sentenced to five years, he was sent to Sing Sing, then to the Dannemora Prison for incorrigibles.

After a couple of months, he made a time bomb and tried to burn down some of the facilities. He tried to escape, but broke his ankles and legs in the attempt.

'Then, I tried to murder a con. I sneaked up behind him as he was sitting in a chair, and I hit him on the back of the head with a ten-pound club. It didn't kill him, but he was good and sick, and he left me alone after that.'

His escape attempt had caused a rupture and he had to have a testicle removed.

'Five days after my operation, when I tried to see if my sexual organs were still in good working order, I got caught trying to commit sodomy on another prisoner.'

One-man crime wave

He was thrown out of the hospital and sent to the Segregation Block, where he spent the remains of his sentence in isolation, and was then released.

'Eighteen days later, I committed six or eight burglaries and, two days later, I committed a murder in Philadelphia, Pennsylvania, A week later I committed a burglary in Baltimore, 12 days later a burglary in Washington, DC. The next day or two, I committed more burglaries in Baltimore, then I was arrested in Baltimore and brought back to Washington, DC.'

He escaped from jail there but was recaptured.

'Here, I am now waiting to see which way the wind blows and perhaps the electric chair, the rope, or the madhouse. It makes very little difference to me either way.'

He reckoned that between the time he had been released from Dannemora on 6 July 1928 and 13 August when he was caught, he committed sodomy about 25 times, burglary 12 times and murder once.

'And I was just getting all set to do a wholesale business in all these lines.'

Expert on torture

A scholar of the methods of Torquemada, the chief inquisitor of the Spanish Inquisition, he spent his time in jail detailing the tortures he had suffered in American prisons.

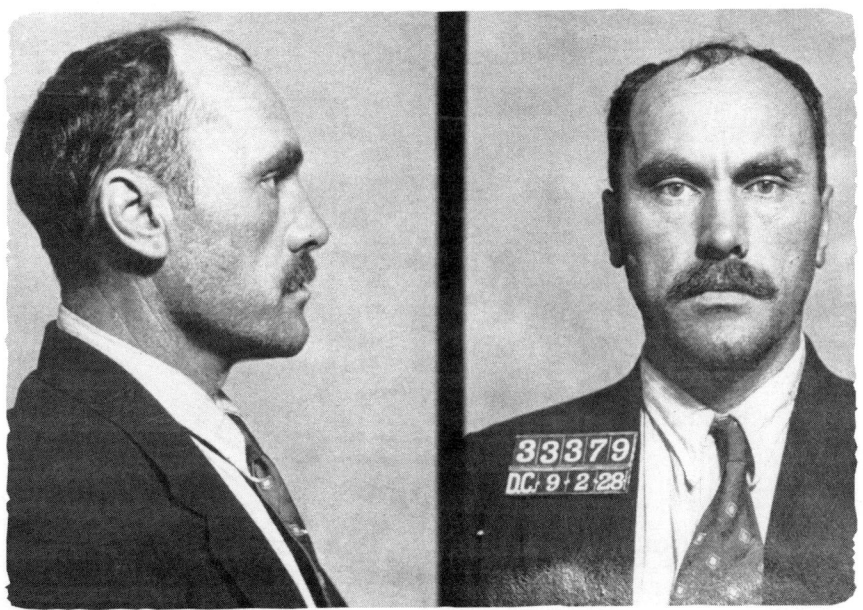

Carl Panzram in 1928.

There was the Humming Bird, where the victim was laid in four or five inches of ice-cold water in a steel bath and a wet sponge connected to a battery was run over his body.

'The sensation of the victim are that there seems to be millions of red-hot needles sticking into him. The agony is intense. Two or three minutes of this and the victim is then all ready for either the grave or madhouse. Yet there is not a single mark or bruise on his whole body.'

The Snorting Pole is a whipping post, where the victim is handcuffed and jacked up until he is on tiptoe. Then his shirt is pulled up and his trousers down, and he is lashed with an eight-foot black snake whip that takes out little chunks of hide.

'If you ever get it, you'll snort the same as I did when I got it. That's why it is called the Snorting Pole... When a man is let down after being well whipped, he has blood on his back and murder in his heart.'

Other whippings were conducted with the victim similarly stripped and held down on the ground. This was known as A Dose of Salts as, after 15 or 20 whacks, 'there is no one around there that is constipated any more'.

The Jacket is a straightforward straitjacket that is tightened with a rope by a burly prison guard.

'After my one hour in the Jacket, my blood had stopped circulating and I was numb all over. When I was taken out, I couldn't walk hardly at all and was not very good for a week. It took more than a month for the effects to wear off... I heard of men who got six to eight hours in the Jacket.'

With the Hose, the victim is stripped naked with his back to the wall, his arms spread and handcuffed. Then he is doused with a regulation fire hose from about 15 feet.

'When I came too, I was nearly blind, all swelled up, from head to foot, ears on the bum for months afterwards, black and blue all over the front of my body; my privates were as big as those of a jackass. The full effects of this didn't ever wear off completely. This is more than ten years ago, but still every time I catch an Oregonian and get him in a corner, I sure give him hell. Many a man has paid for what those men done to me that Sunday morning. Maybe that hose did wash a lot of dirt off the outside of me, but it also washed a hell of a lot of dirt inside of me too.'

In reform school, he suffered the Bat or Paddle, which was an ash stick about 3ft (90 cm) long and 2 in (5 cm) wide. He was stripped naked and laid on a bed, with his arms and legs tied to either end.

'In that position, I got the Bat laid on my back 50 times, put into a cell for ten days, then taken out and given 20 more and then put back into the cell for 20 days more. The first ten days on bread and water, the last 20 on two meals a day, and damned small meals they were too.'

In Leavenworth, he suffered the Restraint Machine several times. Barefoot on a cold, damp concrete floor, he was held against an iron-barred door by a belt pulled tight around his chest. After four hours, he was let down for bread and water. After another four hours, he was let down for morning bread and water, then allowed to sleep on a board with no blankets. This continued for five to 14 days. Then, it was back to nine hours a day swinging an 18 lb (8 kg) sledgehammer busting rocks.

Then there's the Cooler.

'Some are cold and wet. Some are hot and dry. In some, you freeze and in others you roast and sweat. In all, you are hungry and thirsty, filthy and dirty. In some, you stay a day, others a week, and there have been times when I have been in the cooler a month or more. Bread and water isn't very nourishing, and neither does it generate clean thinking in a person's mind. The milk of human kindness generally curdles and turns sour under such conditions. The more Cooler you get, the more heat and hate is generated in your heart.'

Punishing schedule

Panzram asked, 'What is the physical and mental condition of the person while he is undergoing these tortures and how he feels after it is all over and when he is released from prison. Do people think that he forgets all about it and forgives those who do it to him? Oh no… The natural result is that the more of this kind of treatment one gets, the more vindictive he gets. I did and I do.'

In 1928 in Washington, DC, his hands were cuffed behind his back around an iron post. The cuffs and his hands were then pulled up towards the ceiling.

'In that position, I was left for 13 hours one night. The next night, I was first beaten, kicked, choked and blackjacked unconscious and then dragged down and again cuffed up to the Post for a couple more hours. When I was let down, my hands and wrists were swollen to twice their normal size, the skin on my wrists was first blistered and then chaffed thru the meat to the bone…

'All of these things… happened to me, here and now…. The reaction will be revenge by rape, robbery and murder, to me, you and everybody else. It's too late for me to change, but how about you, the Public of this great Land of the Free and the Home of the Brave?'

Panzram warned citizens and taxpayers, 'You pay big taxes to have the privilege of being robbed, raped, and murdered. It costs you thousands of lives and billions of dollars every year to keep on doing business with the present prison and educational systems.'

At 36, with 11 felony convictions behind him, he had spent 20 years in reform schools and prisons.

'If any man ever was a habitual criminal, I am one. In my lifetime, I have broken every law that was ever made by both man and God. If either had made any more, I should very cheerfully have broken them also.'

Hostile to the last

Held in solitary confinement, he dreamed of mass murder, blowing up a train in a tunnel, gassing the passengers, shooting anyone who tried to escape, then stealing anything he could find. Then he would have used the proceeds to go on and steal millions of dollars and kill millions of people by fomenting a war between Britain and the United States.

He also planned mass poisonings.

'I could do a better job than the Borgias done… They didn't kill half enough. They should have killed everybody and left this world for the only good things in it, Nature. This would be a damn fine world if man was out of it. P.S. Hurry up and bring on the electric chair.'

He signed off, saying that he was sorry for only two things.

'I am sorry that I have mistreated some few animals in my lifetime, and I am sorry that I am unable to murder the whole damned human race.'

His was not so much a confession as a declaration of war on humanity. Perhaps we should be grateful that he was hanged on 5 September 1930 before he could put his campaign into practice. When asked by the hangman if he had any last words, he said, 'Yes. Hurry it up, you Hoosier bastard; I could have killed a dozen men all this time you've been screwing around!'

INDEX

PICTURE CREDITS